THE LIFE OF THE BUDDHA

THE LIFE OF THE BUDDHA

TRANSLATED FROM THE PALI

BY

HENRY CLARKE WARREN

GYAN

Published by

Gyan Publishing House
5, Ansari Road
Daryaganj, New Delhi-110002
Phone: 011-47034999, 9811692060
E-mail: books@gyanbooks.com

Distribution Network
gyanbooks.com
India, USA, Canada, UK, Australia, France

ISBN : 978-81-212-3717-8 (PB)

2nd Impression 2020

Printed at: Gyan Press, Delhi.

A Gandhara Buddha from Takht-i-Bahi

See page XI

CHAPTER I.

THE BUDDHA.

CHAPTER I.

THE BUDDHA.

INTRODUCTORY DISCOURSE.

IN reading the Pāli Scriptures one is impressed with the strong personal influence exercised by The Buddha over the hearts of his followers. He was regarded, not as a mere formulator of dry metaphysical propositions, but as a very wise and compassionate friend of his fellow-men. He was full of tact, and all his ways were ways of peace. To allay discord he would tell a little story or fable with a moral, and his epithet for one of whom he disapproved was merely "vain man." Anger, in fact, had no place in his character, and the reader of this book will find that it had equally none in his religio-philosophic system.

The term "Buddha" means "Enlightened One," and signifies that the person to whom it is applied has solved the riddle of existence, and discovered the doctrine for the cessation of misery. It was by his attainment of this supreme "Enlightenment" or Wisdom that Gotama became a Buddha. During the thirty-five years of his life previous to that event, and during all previous existences from the time he set out towards the Buddhaship, he was a Bodhisatta, — a term which I have freely translated "Future Buddha," but which is more literally rendered "He whose essence is Wisdom."

The Buddha's given name would appear to have been Siddhattha; but as the word means "Successful in his Objects," it looks as though it might be a simple epithet. The

Buddha belonged to the Sakya clan. The word "Sakya" means "Powerful;" and the families that bore the name had a reputation for pride and haughtiness. They were of the warrior caste, but cultivated the peaceful arts of agriculture. By his contemporaries The Buddha is usually called Gotama, or, as the word is sometimes Anglicized, the Gotamid. It is not quite clear why he and others of his clan should bear the name of Gotama in addition to that of Sakya. It may be they claimed descent from the ancient sage Gautama (Sanskrit "Gautama" becomes "Gotama" in Pāli), to whom are attributed some of the hymns of the Rig-Veda; or it may be, as Burnouf has suggested, "because Gautama was the sacerdotal family name of the military race of Sakyas, who, being of the warrior caste, had no ancestor or tutelar saint like the Brahmans, but might, as the Hindu law permits, have taken the name of the sage to whose family belonged their spiritual guide."

The Buddha was a Hindu, born not far from the Ganges, and during his long ministry wandered about from place to place in the section of country about Benares, very much as did Christ in Samaria and Judea. And just as Christ once left his native country and went to Egypt, so The Buddha is said by native authorities to have paid a couple of visits to Ceylon; but the statement is, I fear, somewhat mythical.

The date of Gotama Buddha is considered to be the sixth century before Christ. It would appear that he lived to his eightieth year, and the time of his death is given by scholars as about 480 B. C.

The first eight sections of the present chapter are from the general introduction to the Jātaka ("Book of Birth-Stories"). These Birth-Stories, five hundred and fifty in number, are so called because they are tales of the anterior existences of Gotama Buddha, while he was as yet but a

Future Buddha. The Jātaka is an extensive work; five volumes have already been edited by Professor V. Fausböll, of Copenhagen, and more is yet to come. It consists of the Birth-Stories themselves, with a commentary and a long introduction. Examples of these Birth-Stories will be given further on; here we have only to do with the Introduction, the author of which and of the commentary is unknown.

After a few preliminary remarks concerning the inception and plan of his work, the author begins by quoting entire the Story of Sumedha as contained in the metrical work called the Buddha-Vaṁsa ("History of the Buddhas"). He does not quote it all consecutively, but a few stanzas at a time as authority for his prose statements. In this prose is also some matter of a commentary nature, apparently later glosses and not a part of the original text. In my first translation I give the Story of Sumedha as quoted in this Introduction to the Jātaka, but I give it consecutively and omit the prose, except that of some of the more interesting and explanatory passages, of the glosses especially, I have made foot-notes.

After the Story of Sumedha our author gives formal descriptions of each of the twenty-four Buddhas that preceded Gotama. These descriptions, however, are tedious, and are not here translated. They mainly concern themselves with such details as the height of each Buddha, his length of life, how many conversions he made, the names of his father, mother, chief disciples, etc. But from the point where my second section begins to the end of the eighth I follow the native text without making any omissions. I have divided one continuous text into seven parts, and then given these divisions titles of my own devising.

The reader is thus brought up to the ministry of The Buddha. This ministry lasted some forty-five years, and an account of part of it is given by the author of the Introduction. It is, however, only a part that he gives, just enough to conduct his reader up to the time when The Buddha was presented with Jetavana monastery, the importance of which event to our author will be readily perceived when it is remembered that this was the monastery in which The Buddha is represented as having related the greater part of the Birth-Stories. As our author fails to give us a complete life of The Buddha, and as I know of none in Pāli literature, none is attempted in this book. But in order that the reader may have at an early stage an idea of what the matters were wherein The Buddha considered himself "enlightened," two passages are translated from the Mahā-Vagga. Then follows a description of the daily routine of The Buddha's ministry, and the last section of this chapter gives the Pāli account of how The Buddha died. It is not because the philosophical ideas expressed and the references to meditation and trance made in these four sections are supposed to be self-explanatory, that I make no comment on them in this chapter; but because the next three chapters, as I have already stated in my General Introduction, are devoted to the Doctrine, and constitute the philosophical and systematic part of this work. It appeared desirable to give the reader a general idea of what the Buddhists consider to be the salient features of their system of religion before beginning its detailed discussion.

§ 1. THE STORY OF SUMEDHA.[1]

Translated from the Introduction to the Jātaka (i.3[1]).

12. A hundred thousand cycles vast
And four immensities ago,
There was a town named Amara,
A place of beauty and delights.
It had the noises ten complete[2]
And food and drink abundantly.

13. The noise of elephant and horse,
Of conch-shell, drum, and chariot,
And invitations to partake —
"Eat ye, and drink!" — resounded loud.

14. A town complete in all its parts,
Where every industry was found,
And eke the seven precious gems,[3]
And foreigners from many lands.
A prosperous city of the gods,
Full of good works and holy men.

15. Within this town of Amara
Sumedha lived, of Brahman caste,
Who many tens of millions had,
And grain and treasure in full store.

16. A student he, and wise in spells,
A master of the Vedas three.
He fortunes told, tradition knew,
And every duty of his caste.

---

[1] This entire story is related by The Buddha to his disciples, and describes how, in his long-ago existence as the Brahman Sumedha, he first resolved to strive for the Buddhaship. In stanzas 12–16 he speaks of himself, that is, of Sumedha, in the third person, but elsewhere in the first.

[2] Only six of the ten noises indicative of a flourishing town are here mentioned. For the complete list, see p. 101.

[3] Probably gold, silver, pearls, gems (such as sapphire and ruby), cat's-eye, diamond, and coral; or perhaps as given on p. 101, note.

17. In secret then I sat me down,
And thus to ponder I began:
"What misery to be born again!
And have the flesh dissolve at death!

18. "Subject to birth, old age, disease,
Extinction will I seek to find,
Where no decay is ever known,
Nor death, but all security.

19. "What if I now should rid me of
This body foul, this charnel-house,
And go my way without a care,
Or least regret for things behind!

20. "There is, there must be, an escape!
Impossible there should not be!
I'll make the search and find the way,
Which from existence shall release!

21. "Even as, although there misery is,
Yet happiness is also found;
So, though indeed existence is,
A non-existence should be sought.

22. "Even as, although there may be heat,
Yet grateful cold is also found;
So, though the threefold fire[1] exists,
Likewise Nirvana should be sought.

23. "Even as, although there evil is,
That which is good is also found;
So, though 't is true that birth exists,
That which is not birth should be sought.

24. "Even as a man befouled with dung,
Seeing a brimming lake at hand,
And nathless bathing not therein,
Were senseless should he chide the lake;

---

[1] Lust, hatred, and infatuation. Compare page 59, and also the "Fire-sermon," page 351.

25. "So, when Nirvana's lake exists
To wash away corruption's stain,
Should I not seek to bathe therein,
I might not then Nirvana chide.

26. "Even as a man hemmed in by foes,
Seeing a certain safe escape,
And nathless seeking not to flee,
Might not the blameless pathway chide;

27. "So, when my passions hem me in,
And yet a way to bliss exists,
Should I not seek to follow it,
That way of bliss I might not chide.

28. "Even as a man who, sore diseased,
When a physician may be had,
Should fail to send to have him come,
Might the physician then not chide;

29. "So, when diseased with passion, sore
Oppressed, I seek the master not
Whose ghostly counsel me might cure,
The blame should not on him be laid.

30. "Even as a man might rid him of
A horrid corpse bound to his neck,
And then upon his way proceed,
Joyous, and free, and unconstrained;

31. "So must I likewise rid me of
This body foul, this charnel-house,
And go my way without a care,
Or least regret for things behind.

32. "As men and women rid them of
Their dung upon the refuse heap,
And go their ways without a care,
Or least regret for what they leave;

83. "So will I likewise rid me of
This body foul, this charnel-house,
And go my way as if I had
Cast out my filth into the draught.

84. "Even as the owners leave and quit
A worn-out, shattered, leaky ship,
And go their ways without a care,
Or least regret for what they leave;

85. "So will I likewise rid me of
This nine-holed,[1] ever-trickling frame,
And go my way, as owners do,
Who ship disrupted leave behind.

86. "Even as a man who treasure bears,
And finds him in a robber-gang,
Will quickly flee and rid him of
The robbers, lest they steal his gold;

87. "So, to a mighty robber might
Be likened well this body's frame.
I 'll cast it off and go my way,
Lest of my welfare I be robbed."

88. Thus thinking, I on rich and poor
All that I had in alms bestowed;
Hundreds of millions spent I then,
And made to Himavant[2] my way.

89. Not far away from Himavant,
There was a hill named Dhammaka,
And here I made and patterned well
A hermitage and hut of leaves.

---

[1] The two eyes, ears, and so forth, as enumerated at page 298.

[2] The Himalaya mountains. *Himālaya* and *Himavant* are Sanskrit words of almost identical signification. The former means "snow-abode," and is a compound of *hima*, "snow," and *ālaya*, "settling-down place," or "abode." *Hima-vant* means "snow-y."

40. A walking-place I then laid out,
Exempted from the five defects,[1]
And having all the virtues eight;[2]
And there I gained the Six High Powers.

41. Then ceased I cloaks of cloth to wear,
For cloaks possess the nine defects,[3]

---

[1] Native gloss: Jātaka, vol. i., p. 7, l. 14: *Exempted from the five defects:* The following are the five defects in a walking-place: hardness and unevenness; trees in the midst; dense underbrush; excessive narrowness; excessive width. For if the walking-place be on hard and uneven ground, then any one who uses it hurts and blisters his feet, so that he fails of concentration of mind, and his meditation is broken up; while he who walks at ease on a soft and even surface succeeds in meditation. Therefore hardness and unevenness of surface are to be reckoned as one defect. If a walking-place have trees in it, whether in the middle or at the end, then any one who uses it is liable, if not careful, to strike his forehead or his head against them. Therefore trees in the midst are a second defect. If a walking-place be overgrown with a dense underbrush of grass, vines, and so forth, any one who uses it in the dark is liable to tread upon snakes and other creatures and kill them, or they may bite and injure him. Thus a dense underbrush is a third defect. If a walking-place be excessively narrow, say only a cubit or half a cubit wide, then any one who uses it is liable to stumble at the borders and stub his toes and break his toe-nails. Therefore excessive narrowness is a fourth defect. If a walking-place be excessively wide, then any one who uses it is liable to have his mind wander and fail of concentration. Thus excessive width is a fifth defect. A walking-place should be a path a cubit and a half in breadth, with a margin of a cubit on either side, and it should be sixty cubits in length, and it should have a surface soft and evenly sprinkled with sand.

[2] Ibidem, l. 30. *And having all the virtues eight:* Having the eight advantages for a monk. The following are the eight advantages for a monk: it admits of no storing-up of treasure or grain; it favors only a blameless alms-seeking; there one can eat his alms in peace and quiet; there no annoyance is experienced from the reigning families when they oppress the kingdom with their levies of the precious metals or of leaden money; no passionate desire arises for furniture and implements; there is no fear of being plundered by robbers; no intimacies are formed with kings and courtiers; and one is not shut in in any of the four directions.

[3] Native gloss: Jātaka, vol. i., p. 8, l. 27: *For cloaks possess the nine defects:* . . . For one who retires from the world and takes up the life of an anchorite, there are nine defects inherent in garments of cloth. The great cost is one defect; the fact that it is got by dependence on others is another; the fact that it is easily soiled by use is another, for

And girded on a barken dress,
Which is with virtues twelve endued.[1]

42. My hut of leaves I then forsook,
So crowded with the eight defects,[2]
And at the foot of trees I lived,
For such abodes have virtues ten.[3]

---

when it has been soiled it must be washed and dyed; the fact that when it is much worn it must needs be patched and mended is another; the difficulty of obtaining a new one when needed is another; its unsuitableness for an anchorite who has retired from the world is another; its acceptableness to one's enemies is another, for it must needs be guarded lest the enemy take it; the danger that it may be worn for ornament is another; the temptation it affords to load one's self down with it in travelling is another.

[1] The bast, or inner bark of certain trees, was much used in India as cloth, to which indeed it bears a striking resemblance.—Native gloss: Jātaka, vol. i., p. 9, l. 2: *Which is with virtues twelve endued:* Possessing twelve advantages. For there are twelve advantages in a dress of bark. It is cheap, good, and suitable; this is one advantage. You can make it yourself; this is a second. It gets dirty but slowly by use, and hence time is not wasted in washing it; this is a third. It never needs sewing, even when much used and worn; this is a fourth. But when a new one is needed, it can be made with ease; this is a fifth. Its suitableness for an anchorite who has retired from the world is a sixth. That it is of no use to one's enemies is a seventh. That it cannot be worn for ornament is an eighth. Its lightness is a ninth. Its conducing to moderation in dress is a tenth. The irreproachableness and blamelessness of searching for bark is an eleventh. And the unimportance of its loss is a twelfth.

[2] Native gloss: Jātaka, vol. i., p. 9, l. 11: *My hut of leaves I then forsook, So crowded with the eight defects:* . . . (L. 36) For there are eight evils connected with the use of a leaf-hut. The great labor involved in searching for materials and in the putting of them together is one evil. The constant care necessary to replace the grass, leaves, and bits of clay that fall down is a second. Houses may do for old men, but no concentration of mind is possible when one's meditation is liable to be interrupted; thus the liability to interruption is a third. The protection afforded against heat and cold renders the body delicate, and this is a fourth. In a house all sorts of evil deeds are possible; thus the cover it affords for disgraceful practices is a fifth. The taking possession, saying, "This is mine," is a sixth. To have a house is like having a companion; this is a seventh. And the sharing of it with many others, as for instance with lice, bugs, and house-lizards, is an eighth.

[3] Ibidem, p. 10, l. 9: *And at the foot of trees I lived, For such abodes have virtues ten;* . . . The following are the ten virtues. The smallness of

43. No sown and cultivated grain
Allowed I then to be my food;
But all the many benefits
Of wild-fruit fare I made my own.

44. And strenuous effort made I there,
The while I sat, or stood, or walked;
And ere seven days had passed away,
I had attained the Powers High.

45. When I had thus success attained,
And made me master of the Law,
A Conqueror, Lord of All the World,
Was born, by name Dīpaṁkara.

46. What time he was conceived, was born,
What time he Buddhaship attained,
When first he preached, — the Signs[1] appeared.
I saw them not, deep sunk in trance.

47. Then, in the distant border-land,
Invited they this Being Great,
And every one, with joyful heart,
The pathway for his coming cleared.

---

the undertaking is one virtue, for all that is necessary is simply to go to the tree. The small amount of care it requires is a second; for, whether swept or unswept, it is suitable for use. The freedom from interruption is a third. It affords no cover for disgraceful practices; wickedness there would be too public; thus the fact that it affords no cover for disgraceful practices is a fourth. It is like living under the open sky, for there is no feeling that the body is confined; thus the non-confinement of the body is a fifth. There is no taking possession; this is a sixth. The abandonment of all longings for household life is a seventh. When a house is shared with others, some one is liable to say, "I will look after this house myself. Begone!" Thus the freedom from eviction is an eighth. The happy contentment experienced by the occupant is a ninth. The little concern one need feel about lodgings, seeing that a man can find a tree no matter where he may be stopping, — this is a tenth.

[1] Translated from the prose of the Jātaka, vol. i., p. 10, last line but one: At his [Dīpaṁkara's] conception, birth, attainment of Buddhaship, and when he caused the Wheel of Doctrine to roll, the entire system of ten thousand worlds trembled, quivered, and shook, and roared with a mighty roar; also the Thirty-Two Prognostics appeared. [For the Thirty-Two Prognostics, see page 44.]

48. Now so it happened at this time,
That I my hermitage had left,
And, barken garments rustling loud,
Was passing o'er them through the air.

49. Then saw I every one alert,
Well-pleased, delighted, overjoyed;
And, coming downward from the sky,
The multitude I straightway asked:

50. "Well-pleased, delighted, overjoyed,
And all alert is every one;
For whom is being cleared the way,
The path, the track to travel on?"

51. When thus I asked, response was made:
"A mighty Buddha has appeared,
A Conqueror, Lord of All the World,
Whose name is called Dīpaṁkara.
For him is being cleared the way,
The path, the track to travel on."

52. This word, "The Buddha," when I heard,
Joy sprang up straightway in my heart;
"A Buddha! Buddha!" cried I then,
And publishèd my heart's content.

53. And standing there I pondered deep,
By joyous agitation seized:
"Here will I now some good seed sow,
Nor let this fitting season slip."

54. "For a Buddha do ye clear the road?
Then, pray, grant also me a place!
I, too, will help to clear the way,
The path, the track to travel on."

55. And so they granted also me
A portion of the path to clear,
And I gan clear, while still my heart
Said "Buddha! Buddha!" o'er and o'er.

56. But ere my part was yet complete,
Dīpaṁkara, the Mighty Sage,
The Conqueror, came that way along,
Thronged by four hundred thousand saints,
Without depravity or spot,
And having each the Six High Powers.

57. The people then their greetings gave,
And many kettle-drums were beat,
And men and gods, in joyous mood,
Loud shouted their applauding cries.

58. Then men and gods together met,
And saw each other face to face;
And all with joinèd hands upraised
Followed The Buddha and his train.

59. The gods, with instruments divine,
The men, with those of human make,
Triumphant music played, the while
They followed in The Buddha's train.

60. Celestial beings from on high
Threw broadcast over all the earth
The Erythrina flowers of heaven,
The lotus and the coral-flower.

61. And men abiding on the ground
On every side flung up in air
Champakas, salaḷas, nīpas,
Nāgas, punnāgas, ketakas.

62. Then loosened I my matted hair,
And, spreading out upon the mud
My dress of bark and cloak of skin,
I laid me down upon my face.

63. "Let now on me The Buddha tread,
With the disciples of his train;
Can I but keep him from the mire,
To me great merit shall accrue."

64. While thus I lay upon the ground,[1]
Arose within me many thoughts:
"To-day, if such were my desire,
I my corruptions might consume.

65. "But why thus in an unknown guise
Should I the Doctrine's fruit secure?
Omniscience first will I achieve,
And be a Buddha in the world.

66. "Or why should I, a valorous man,
The ocean seek to cross alone?
Omniscience first will I achieve,
And men and gods convey across.

67. "Since now I make this earnest wish,
In presence of this Best of Men,
Omniscience sometime I'll achieve,
And multitudes convey across.

68. "I'll rebirth's circling stream arrest,
Destroy existence's three modes;
I'll climb the sides of Doctrine's ship,
And men and gods convey across.

69. "A human being,[2] male of sex,
Who saintship gains, a Teacher meets,
As hermit lives, and virtue loves,
Nor lacks resolve, nor fiery zeal,
Can by these eight conditions joined,
Make his most earnest wish succeed."

---

[1] Native gloss: Jātaka, vol. i., p. 13, l. 31: As he lay in the mud, he opened his eyes again, and gazing upon the Buddha-glory of Dipaṁkara, The Possessor of the Ten Forces, he reflected as follows: "If I so wished, I might burn up all my corruptions, and as novice follow with the congregation when they enter the city of Ramma; but I do not want to burn up my corruptions and enter Nirvana unknown to any one. What now if I, like Dipaṁkara, were to acquire the supreme wisdom, were to cause multitudes to go on board the ship of Doctrine and cross the ocean of the round of rebirth, and were afterwards to pass into Nirvana! That would be something worthy of me!"

[2] Native gloss: Jātaka, vol. i., p. 14, l. 20: For it is only a human being that can successfully wish to be a Buddha; a serpent, or a bird,

70. Dīpaṁkara, Who Knew All Worlds,
Recipient of Offerings,
Came to a halt my pillow near,
And thus addressed the multitudes:

71. "Behold ye now this monk austere,
His matted locks, his penance fierce!
Lo! he, unnumbered cycles hence,
A Buddha in the world shall be.

---

or a deity cannot successfully make the wish. Of human beings it is only one of the male sex that can make the wish: it would not be successful on the part of a woman, or of a eunuch, or of a neuter, or of a hermaphrodite. Of men it is he, and only he, who is in a fit condition by the attainment of saintship in that same existence, that can successfully make the wish. Of those in a fit condition it is only he who makes the wish in the presence of a living Buddha that succeeds in his wish; after the death of a Buddha a wish made at a relic-shrine, or at the foot of a Bo-tree, will not be successful. Of those who make the wish in the presence of a Buddha it is he, and only he, who has retired from the world that can successfully make the wish, and not one who is a layman. Of those who have retired from the world it is only he who is possessed of the Five High Powers and is master of the Eight Attainments that can successfully make the wish, and no one can do so who is lacking in these excellences. Of those, even, who possess these excellences it is he, and only he, who has such firm resolve that he is ready to sacrifice his life for The Buddhas that can successfully make the wish, but no other. Of those who possess this resolve it is he, and only he, who has great zeal, determination, strenuousness, and endeavor in striving for the qualities that make a Buddha that is successful. The following comparisons will show the intensity of the zeal. If he is such a one as to think: "The man who, if all within the rim of the world were to become water, would be ready to swim across it with his own arms and get to the further shore, — he is the one to attain the Buddhaship; or, in case all within the rim of the world were to become a jungle of bamboo, would be ready to elbow and trample his way through it and get to the further side, — he is the one to attain the Buddhaship; or, in case all within the rim of the world were to become a *terra firma* of thick-set javelins, would be ready to tread on them and go afoot to the further side, — he is the one to attain the Buddhaship; or, in case all within the rim of the world were to become live coals, would be ready to tread on them and so get to the further side, — he is the one to attain the Buddhaship," — if he deems not even one of these feats too hard for himself, but has such great zeal, determination, strenuousness, and power of endeavor that he would perform these feats in order to attain the Buddhaship, then, but not otherwise, will his wish succeed.

72. "From the fair town called Kapila
His Great Retirement shall be made.
Then, when his Struggle fierce is o'er,
His stern austerities performed, —

73. "He shall in quiet sit him down
Beneath the Ajapāla-tree;
There pottage made of rice receive,
And seek the stream Nerañjarā.

74. "This pottage shall The Conqueror eat,
Beside the stream Nerañjarā,
And thence by road triumphal go
To where the Tree of Wisdom stands.

75. "Then shall the Peerless, Glorious One
Walk to the right, round Wisdom's Throne,
And there The Buddhaship achieve,
While sitting at the fig-tree's root.

76. "The mother that shall bring him forth,
Shall Māyā callèd be by name;
Suddhodana his father's name;
His own name shall be Gotama.

77. "Kolita, Upatissa[1] too, —
These shall his Chief Disciples be;
Both undepraved, both passion-free,
And tranquil and serene of mind.

78. "Ānanda shall be servitor
And on The Conqueror attend;
Khemā and Uppalavaṇṇā
Shall female Chief Disciples be,

79. "Both undepraved, both passion-free,
And tranquil and serene of mind.
The Bo-tree of this Blessed One
Shall be the tree Assattha[1] called."

---

[1] Better known as Moggallāna and Sāriputta, respectively.
[2] Ficus religiosa.

80. Thus spake Th' Unequalled, Mighty Sage;
And all, when they had heard his speech,
Both men and gods rejoiced, and said:
"Behold a Buddha-scion here!"

81. Now shouts were heard on every side,
The people clapped their arms and laughed.
Ten thousand worlds of men and gods
Paid me their homage then and said:

82. "If of our Lord Dīpaṁkara
The Doctrine now we fail to grasp,
We yet shall stand in time to come
Before this other face to face.

83. "Even as, when men a river cross,
And miss th' opposing landing-place,
A lower landing-place they find,
And there the river-bank ascend;

84. "Even so, we all, if we let slip
The present Conqueror that we have,
Yet still shall stand in time to come
Before this other, face to face."

85. Dīpaṁkara, Who All Worlds Knew,
Recipient of Offerings,
My future having prophesied,
His right foot raised and went his way.

86. And all who were this Conqueror's sons,
Walked to the right around me then;
And serpents, men, and demigods,
Saluting me, departed thence.

87. Now when The Leader of the World
Had passed from sight with all his train,
My mind with rapturous transport filled,
I raised me up from where I lay.

88. Then overjoyed with joy was I,
Delighted with a keen delight;
And thus with pleasure saturate
I sat me down with legs across.

89. And while cross-leggèd there I sat,
I thus reflected to myself:
"Behold! in trance am I adept,
And all the Powers High are mine.

90. "Nowhere throughout a thousand worlds
Are any seers to equal me;
Unequalled in the magic gifts
Have I this height of bliss attained."

91. Now while I sat with legs across,
The dwellers of ten thousand worlds
Rolled forth a glad and mighty shout:[1]
"Surely a Buddha thou shalt be!

92. "The presages that erst were seen,
When Future Buddhas sat cross-legged,
These presages are seen to-day—
Surely a Buddha thou shalt be!

93. "All cold is everywhere dispelled,
And mitigated is the heat;
These presages are seen to-day—
Surely a Buddha thou shalt be!

94. "The system of ten thousand worlds
Is hushed to quiet and to peace;
These presages are seen to-day—
Surely a Buddha thou shalt be!

---

[1] There have been many beings who, like Sumedha here, were to become Buddhas, and who were therefore called Bodhi-sattas or "Future Buddhas." The certainty of their ultimate "Illumination," or Buddhaship, was always foretokened by certain presages. The "dwellers of ten thousand worlds" describe in the following stanzas what these presages were, declare that they are reappearing now, and announce to Sumedha their prophetic inference that he will attain Buddhaship.

95. "The mighty winds then cease to blow,
Nor do the rivers onward glide;
These presages are seen to-day —
Surely a Buddha thou shalt be!

96. "All plants, be they of land or stream,
Do straightway put their blossoms forth;
Even so to-day they all have bloomed —
Surely a Buddha thou shalt be!

97. "And every tree, and every vine,
Is straightway laden down with fruit;
Even so to-day they're laden down —
Surely a Buddha thou shalt be!

98. "In sky and earth doth straightway then
Full many a radiant gem appear;
Even so to-day they shine afar —
Surely a Buddha thou shalt be!

99. "Then straightway music's heard to play
'Mongst men on earth and gods in heaven;
So all to-day in music join —
Surely a Buddha thou shalt be!

100. "There falleth straightway down from heaven
A rain of many-colored flowers;
Even so to-day these flowers are seen —
Surely a Buddha thou shalt be!

101. "The mighty ocean heaves and roars,
And all the worlds ten thousand quake;
Even so is now this tumult heard —
Surely a Buddha thou shalt be!

102. "Straightway throughout the whole of hell
The fires ten thousand all die out;
Even so to-day have all expired —
Surely a Buddha thou shalt be!

103. "Unclouded then the sun shines forth,
And all the stars appear to view;
Even so to-day do they appear—
Surely a Buddha thou shalt be!

104. "Straightway, although no rain hath fallen,
Burst springs of water from the earth;
Even so to-day they gush in streams—
Surely a Buddha thou shalt be!

105 "And bright then shine the starry hosts
And constellations in the sky;
The moon in Libra now doth stand—
Surely a Buddha thou shalt be!

106. "All beasts that lurk in holes and clefts,
Then get them forth from out their lairs;
Even so to-day they've left their dens—
Surely a Buddha thou shalt be!

107. "Straightway content is all the world,
And no unhappiness is known;
Even so to-day are all content—
Surely a Buddha thou shalt be!

108. "Then every sickness vanishes,
And hunger likewise disappears;
These presages are seen to-day—
Surely a Buddha thou shalt be!

109. "Then lust doth dwindle and grow weak,
And hate, infatuation too;
Even so to-day they disappear—
Surely a Buddha thou shalt be!

110. "Then fear and danger are unknown;
All we are freed from them to-day;
And by this token we perceive—
'Surely a Buddha thou shalt be!'

111. "No dust upwhirleth towards the sky;
Even so to-day this thing is seen;
And by this token we perceive—
'Surely a Buddha thou shalt be!'

112. "All noisome odors drift away,
And heavenly fragrance fills the air;
Even so the winds now sweetness waft—
Surely a Buddha thou shalt be!

113. "Then all the gods appear to view,
Save those that hold the formless realm;
Even so to-day these all are seen—
Surely a Buddha thou shalt be!

114. "Then clearly seen are all the hells,
However many be their tale;
Even so to-day may all be seen—
Surely a Buddha thou shalt be!

115. "Through walls, and doors, and mountain-rocks,
One finds an easy passage then;
Even so to-day they yield like air—
Surely a Buddha thou shalt be!

116. "Existence then forbears its round
Of death and rebirth for a time;
Even so to-day this thing is seen—
Surely a Buddha thou shalt be!

117. "Do thou a strenuous effort make!
Do not turn back! Go on! Advance!
Most certainly we know this thing:
'Surely a Buddha thou shalt be!'"

118. When I had heard The Buddha's speech,
And what the worlds ten thousand said,
Well-pleased, delighted, overjoyed,
I thus reflected to myself:

119. "The Buddhas never liars are;
A Conqueror's word ne'er yet was vain;
Nothing but truth The Buddhas speak —
Surely a Buddha I shall be!

120. "As clods thrown upward in the air
Fall surely back upon the earth,
So what the glorious Buddhas speak
Is sure and steadfast to the end.
Nothing but truth The Buddhas speak[1] —
Surely a Buddha I shall be![1]

121. "As also for each living thing
The approach of death is ever sure,
So what the glorious Buddhas speak
Is sure and steadfast to the end.
Nothing but truth The Buddhas speak[1] —
Surely a Buddha I shall be![1]

122. "As at the waning of the night
The rising of the sun is sure,
So what the glorious Buddhas speak
Is sure and steadfast to the end.
Nothing but truth, *etc.*[1]

123. "As, when he issues from his den,
The roaring of the lion's sure,
So what the glorious Buddhas speak
Is sure and steadfast to the end.
Nothing but truth, *etc.*[1]

124. "As when a female has conceived,
Her bringing forth of young is sure,
So what the glorious Buddhas speak
Is sure and steadfast to the end.
Nothing but truth The Buddhas speak[1] —
Surely a Buddha I shall be![1]

---

[1] This refrain is added to these stanzas in the Buddha-Vaṁsa. In the Jātaka it is omitted.

125. "Come now! I'll search that I may find
Conditions which a Buddha make —
Above, below, to all ten[1] points,
Where'er conditions hold their sway."

126. And then I searched, and saw the First
Perfection, which consists in Alms,
That highroad great whereon of old
The former seers had ever walked.

127. "Come now! This one as first adopt,
And practise it determinedly;
Acquire perfection in thine Alms,
If thou to Wisdom wouldst attain.

128. "As when a jar is brimming full,
And some one overturneth it,
The jar its water all gives forth,
And nothing for itself keeps back;

129. "So, when a suppliant thou dost see,
Of mean, or high, or middling rank,
Give all in Alms, in nothing stint,
E'en as the overturnèd jar.

130. "But now there must be more than these
Conditions which a Buddha make:
Still others will I seek to find
That shall in Buddhaship mature."

131. Perfection Second then I sought,
And lo! the Precepts came to view,
Which mighty seers of former times
Had practised and had follow'd.

132. "Come now! as second this adopt,
And practise it determinedly;
The Precepts to perfection keep,
If thou to Wisdom wouldst attain.

---

1 The four cardinal points of the compass, the four intermediate points, the zenith and nadir.

133. "As when a Yak cow's flowing tail
Is firmly caught by bush or thorn,
She thereupon awaits her death,
But will not tear and mar her tail;[1]

134. "So likewise thou in stages four,
Observe and keep the Precepts whole,
On all occasions guard them well,
As ever Yak cow does her tail.

135. "But now there must be more than these
Conditions which a Buddha make;
Still others will I seek to find
That shall in Buddhaship mature."

136. And then Perfection Third I sought,
Which is Renunciation called,
Which mighty seers of former times
Had practised and had follow'd.

137. "Come now! this one as third adopt,
And practise it determinedly;
Renounce, and in perfection grow,
If thou to Wisdom wouldst attain.

138. "Even as a man who long has dwelt
In prison, suffering miserably,
No liking for the place conceives,
But only longeth for release;

139. "So likewise thou must every mode
Of being as a prison view—
Renunciation be thy aim;
Thus from existence free thyself.

140. "But now there must be more than these
Conditions which a Buddha make;
Still others will I seek to find
That shall in Buddhaship mature."

---

[1] As Fausböll observes, a very similar statement is made by Aelian, περὶ ζώων, xvi. 11. See also Visuddhi-Magga, chapter i.

141. And then I sought and found the Fourth
Perfection, which is Wisdom called,
Which mighty seers of former times
Had practised and had follow'd.

142. "Come now! this one as fourth adopt,
And practise it determinedly;
Wisdom to its perfection bring,
If thou to Wisdom wouldst attain.

143. "Just as a priest, when on his rounds,
Nor low, nor high, nor middling folk
Doth shun, but begs of every one,
And so his daily food receives;

144. "So to the learned ay resort,
And seek thy Wisdom to increase;
And when this Fourth Perfection's gained,
A Buddha's Wisdom shall be thine.

145. "But now there must be more than these
Conditions which a Buddha make;
Still others will I seek to find
That shall in Buddhaship mature."

146. And then I sought and found the Fifth
Perfection, which is Courage called,
Which mighty seers of former times
Had practised and had follow'd.

147. "Come now! this one as fifth adopt,
And practise it determinedly;
In Courage perfect strive to be,
If thou to Wisdom wouldst attain.

148. "Just as the lion, king of beasts,
In crouching, walking, standing still,
With courage ever is instinct,
And watchful always, and alert;

149. "So thou in each repeated birth,
Courageous energy display;
And when this Fifth Perfection 's gained,
A Buddha's Wisdom shall be thine.

150. "But now there must be more than these
Conditions which a Buddha make;
Still others will I seek to find
That shall in Buddhaship mature."

151. And then I sought and found the Sixth
Perfection, which is Patience called,
Which mighty seers of former times
Had practised and had follow'd.

152. "Come now! this one as sixth adopt,
And practise it determinedly;
And if thou keep an even mood,
A Buddha's Wisdom shall be thine.

153. "Just as the earth, whate'er is thrown
Upon her, whether sweet or foul,
All things endures, and never shows
Repugnance, nor complacency;

154. "E'en so, or honor thou, or scorn,
Of men, with patient mood must bear;
And when this Sixth Perfection 's gained,
A Buddha's Wisdom shall be thine.

155. "But now there must be more than these
Conditions which a Buddha make;
Still others will I seek to find
That shall in Buddhaship mature."

156. And then I sought and found the Seventh
Perfection, which is that of Truth,
Which mighty seers of former times
Had practised and had follow'd.

157. "Come now! this one as seventh adopt,
And practise it determinedly;
If thou art ne'er of double speech,
A Buddha's Wisdom shall be thine.

158. "Just as the morning star on high
Its balanced course doth ever keep,
And through all seasons, times, and years,
Doth never from its pathway swerve;

159. "So likewise thou in all thy speech
Swerve never from the path of truth;
And when this Seventh Perfection 's gained,
A Buddha's Wisdom shall be thine.

160. "But now there must be more than these
Conditions which a Buddha make;
Still others will I seek to find
That shall in Buddhaship mature."

161. And then I sought and found the Eighth
Perfection, Resolution called,
Which mighty seers of former times
Had practised and had follow'd.

162. "Come now! this one as eighth adopt,
And practise it determinedly;
And when thou art immovable,
A Buddha's Wisdom shall be thine.

163. "Just as a rocky mountain-peak,
Unmovèd stands, firm-stablishèd,
Unshaken by the boisterous gales,
And always in its place abides;

164. "So likewise thou must ever be
In Resolution firm intrenched;
And when this Eighth Perfection 's gained,
A Buddha's Wisdom shall be thine.

165. "But now there must be more than these
Conditions which a Buddha make;
Still others will I seek to find
That shall in Buddhaship mature."

166. And then I sought and found the Ninth
Perfection, which is called Good-will;
Which mighty seers of former times
Had practised and had follow'd.

167. "Come now! this one as ninth adopt,
And practise it determinedly;
Unequalled be in thy Good-will,
If thou to Wisdom wouldst attain.

168. "As water cleanseth all alike,
The righteous and the wicked, too,
From dust and dirt of every kind,
And with refreshing coolness fills;

169. "So likewise thou both friend and foe,
Alike with thy Good-will refresh,
And when this Ninth Perfection 's gained,
A Buddha's Wisdom shall be thine.

170. "But now there must be more than these
Conditions which a Buddha make;
Still others will I seek to find
That shall in Buddhaship mature."

171. And then I sought and found the Tenth
Perfection, called Indifference;
Which mighty seers of former times
Had practised and had follow'd.

172. "Come now! this one as tenth adopt,
And practise it determinedly;
And when thou art of equal poise,
A Buddha's Wisdom shall be thine.

173. "Just as the earth, whate'er is thrown
Upon her, whether sweet or foul,
Indifferent is to all alike,
Nor hatred shows, nor amity;

174. "So likewise thou in good or ill,
Must even-balanced ever be;
And when this Tenth Perfection's gained,
A Buddha's Wisdom shall be thine.

175. "But earth no more conditions hath
That in The Buddhaship mature;
Beyond these are there none to seek;
So practise these determinedly."

176. Now pondering these conditions ten,
Their nature, essence, character, —
Such fiery vigor had they all,
That all the worlds ten thousand quaked.

177. Then shook and creaked the wide, wide earth,
As doth the sugar-mill at work;
Then quaked the ground, as doth the wheel
Of oil-mills when they're made to turn.

178. Th' entire assemblage that was there,
And followed in The Buddha's train,
Trembled and shook in great alarm,
And fell astonied to the ground.

179. And many thousand waterpots,
And many hundred earthen jars,
Were one upon another dashed,
And crushed and pounded into dust.

180. Excited, trembling, terrified,
Confused, and sore oppressed in mind,
The multitudes together came,
And to Dīpaṁkara approached.

181. "Oh, tell us what these signs portend.
Will good or ill betide the world?
Lo! terror seizes hold on all.
Dispel our fears, All-Seeing One!"

182. The Great Sage, then, Dīpaṁkara,
Allayed and pacified their fears:—
"Be comforted; and fear ye not
For that the world doth quake and shake.

183. "Of whom to-day I made proclaim—
'A glorious Buddha shall he be,'—
He now conditions pondereth,
Which former Conquerors fulfilled.

184. "'T is while on these he is intent,
As basis for The Buddhaship,
The ground in worlds ten thousand shakes,
In all the realms of gods and men."

185. When thus they'd heard The Buddha speak,
Their anxious minds received relief;
And all then drawing near to me,
Again they did me reverence.

186. Thus on the road to Buddhaship,
And firm determined in my mind,
I raised me up from off my seat,
And reverenced Dīpaṁkara.

187. Then as I raised me from my seat,
Both gods and men in unison
Sweet flowers of heaven and flowers of earth
Profusely sprinkled on my head.

188. And gods and men in unison
Their great delight proclaimed aloud:—
"A mighty prayer thou now hast made;
Succeed according to thy wish!

189. "From all misfortunes be thou free,
Let every sickness disappear!

Mayst thou no hindrance ever know,
And highest Wisdom soon achieve!

190. "As, when the time of spring has come,
The trees put forth their buds and flowers,
Likewise dost thou, O Hero Great,
With knowledge of a Buddha bloom.

191. "As all they who have Buddhas been,
The Ten Perfections have fulfilled,
Likewise do thou, O Hero Great,
The Ten Perfections strive to gain.

192. "As all they who have Buddhas been,
On Wisdom's Throne their insight gained,
Likewise do thou, O Hero Great,
On Conqueror's Throne thy insight gain.

193. "As all they who have Buddhas been,
Have made the Doctrine's Wheel to roll,
Likewise do thou, O Hero Great,
Make Doctrine's Wheel to roll once more.

194. "As on the mid-day of the month
The moon in full perfection shines,
Likewise do thou, with perfect mind,
Shine brightly in ten thousand worlds.

195. "As when the sun, by Rāhu freed,
Shines forth exceeding bright and clear,
So thou, when freed from ties of earth,
Shine forth in bright magnificence.

196. "Just as the rivers of all lands
Into the ocean find their way,
May gods and men from every world
Approach and find their way to thee."

197. Thus praised they me with glad acclaim;
And I, beginning to fulfil
The ten conditions of my quest,
Re-entered then into the wood.

END OF THE STORY OF SUMEDHA.

§ 2. A LIST OF FORMER BUDDHAS.

Translated from the Introduction to the Jātaka (i.43[28]).

Now in the same world-cycle that saw Dīpaṁkara, The One Possessing the Ten Forces, there were also three other Buddhas; but as none of them prophesied concerning the Future Buddha, I have not mentioned them. In the Commentary, however, all the Buddhas are mentioned from the beginning of that world-cycle on, as follows: —

247. "Taṇhaṁkara, Medhaṁkara,
And also Saraṇaṁkara,
Dīpaṁkara, the Buddha great,
Koṇḍañña, of all men the chief,

248. "Maṅgala, and Sumana too,
Revata, Sobhita, the sage,
Anomadassi, Paduma,
Nārada, Padumuttara,

249. "Sumedha, and Sujāta too,
Piyadassi, the glorious one,
Atthadassi, Dhammadassi,
Siddhattha, guide of every man,

250. "Tissa, Phussa, the Buddha great,
Vipassi, Sikkhi, Vessabhū,
Kakusandha, Konāgamana,
Kassapa also, guide for men, —

251. "All these aforetime Buddhas were,
Tranquil, from every passion free.
And like the sun, the many-rayed,
They chased away the darkness dense,
And having flamed like tongues of fire,
Became extinct with all their train."

Our Future Buddha, in his passage through four immensities and a hundred thousand world-cycles to the present time, has made his wish under twenty-four of these Buddhas, beginning with Dīpaṁkara. But since Kassapa, The Blessed One, there has been no Supreme Buddha excepting our present one. Accordingly, our Future Buddha has received recognition at the hands of twenty-four Buddhas, beginning with Dīpaṁkara.

---

§ 3. THE CHARACTERISTICS OF A FUTURE BUDDHA.

Translated from the Introduction to the Jātaka (i.44[20]).

> "A human being, male of sex,
> Who saintship gains, a Teacher meets,
> As hermit lives, and virtue loves,
> Nor lacks resolve, nor fiery zeal,
> Can by these eight conditions joined,
> Make his most earnest wish succeed."

These eight conditions were all united in him when he made his earnest wish at the feet of Dīpaṁkara, saying, —

> "Come now! I'll search that I may find
> Conditions which a Buddha make."

Thereupon, putting forth a strenuous effort, — as it is said, —

> "And then I searched, and found the First
> Perfection, which consists in alms," —

he discovered, not only the perfection which is called alms, but also all the others that go to make a Buddha. And in fulfilling them he reached his Vessantara existence.[1] In so doing, all the blessings celebrated in the following stanzas as belonging to Future Buddhas who make the earnest wish were attained by him: —

---

[1] The Vessantara Birth-Story is the last of the five hundred and fifty, and is not yet published.

252. "Such men in every virtue trained,
And destined for the Buddhaship,
In all their weary rounds of birth,
Though cycle-millions come and go,

253. "Are never born inside of hell,
Nor in the intermundane voids.
They never share the Manes' thirst,[1]
Their hunger or ferocity,[1]
And though sometimes of low estate,
Are never of the insect class.

254. "When they appear among mankind,
'T is not as blind from birth they come,
Deafness they never have to bear,
Nor dumbness have they to endure.

255. "They 're never of the female sex,
Nor as hermaphrodites appear,
As eunuchs are they never classed,
Those destined for the Buddhaship.

256. "From all the five great crimes exempt,
And pure in all their walks in life,
They follow not vain heresy,
For well they know how karma works.

257. "Though in the heavens they may be born,
Yet ne'er 'mongst those perception-reft;
Nor are they destined to rebirth
'Mongst dwellers in the Pure Abodes.[2]

258. "These pleasure-abnegating men
Live unattached in every birth,
And ever toil to help the world,
While all perfections they fulfil."

---

[1] I despair of giving in metre more than the general drift of these two lines. See Hardy, "Manual of Budhism," chap. ii. § 11.

[2] See page 289.

Now in accomplishing these Ten Perfections there was no limit to the number of existences in which he fulfilled the perfection of almsgiving; as when he was born as the Brahman Akitti, the Brahman Saṁkha, king Dhanañjaya, Mahā-Sudassana, Mahā-Govinda, king Nimi, prince Canda, Visayha the treasurer, king Sivi, and king Vessantara. But the acme was reached when as the Wise Hare[1] he said, —

259. "There came a beggar, asked for food;
Myself I gave that he might eat.
In alms there's none can equal me;
In alms have I perfection reached."

Thus, in this offering up of his own life, he acquired the perfection of almsgiving in its highest degree.

Likewise there was no limit to the number of existences in which he fulfilled the precepts; as when he was born as the elephant-king Sīlava, the snake-king Campeyya, the snake-king Bhūridatta, the elephant-king Chaddanta, and prince Alīnasattu, son of king Jayaddisa. But the acme was reached when, as related in the Saṁkhapāla Birth-Story, he said, —

260. "They pierced me through with pointed stakes,
They hacked me with their hunting-knives;
Yet gainst these Bhojans raged I not,
But kept the precepts perfectly."

Thus, in giving up his own life, he acquired perfection in the keeping of the precepts.

Likewise there was no limit to the number of existences in which he fulfilled the perfection of abnegation by aban-

[1] The story of the Future Buddha's existence as the Wise Hare is given further on under the caption, "The Hare-Mark in the Moon." It is the only one of the numerous Birth-Stories above-mentioned that is to be found in this book. The stanza quoted, however, is not taken from that account, but from another work called the Cariyā-Piṭaka, which is wholly in poetry. The Cariyā-Piṭaka consists of Birth-Stories, and, besides the Wise Hare, gives several others of those here mentioned. Some are also briefly alluded to in the ninth chapter of the Visuddhi-Magga; but of course the great treasure-house for Birth-Stories is the Jātaka itself.

doning his throne; as when he was born as prince Somanassa, prince Hatthipāla, and the pandit Ayoghara. But the acme was reached when, as related in the Lesser Sutasoma Birth-Story, he said, —

> 261. "A kingdom dropped into my hands;
> Like spittle vile I let it fall,
> Nor for it felt the smallest wish,
> And thus renunciation gained."

Thus, free from attachment, he renounced a kingdom and retired from the world, and by so doing acquired the perfection of abnegation in its highest degree.

Likewise there was no limit to the number of existences in which he fulfilled the perfection of knowledge; as when he was born as the pandit Vidhūra, the pandit Mahā-Govinda, the pandit Kuddāla, the pandit Araka, the wandering ascetic Bodhi, and the pandit Mahosadha. But the acme was reached when, as the pandit Senaka of the Sattubhatta Birth-Story, he said, —

> 262. "With wisdom sifted I the case,
> And freed the Brahman from his woe;
> In wisdom none can equal me:
> In wisdom I've perfection reached,"

and displayed to all present the serpent which lay concealed in the bag, and in so doing acquired the perfection of wisdom in its highest degree.

Likewise there was no limit to the number of existences in which he fulfilled the perfection of courage. But the acme was reached when, as related in the Greater Janaka Birth-Story, he said, —

> 263. "Far out of sight of land were we,
> The crew were all as dead of fright;
> Yet still unruffled was my mind:
> In courage I've perfection reached."

Thus it was in crossing the ocean he acquired the perfection of courage in its highest degree.

Likewise in the Khantivāda Birth-Story, where he said, —

264. "Like one insensible I lay,
While with his hatchet keen he hacked,
Nor raged I gainst Benares' king:
In patience I've perfection reached,"

in enduring great suffering, while appearing to be unconscious, he acquired the perfection of patience in its highest degree.

Likewise in the Greater Sutasoma Birth-Story, where he said, —

265. "I kept the promise I had made,
And gave my life in sacrifice,
A hundred warriors set I free:
In truth have I perfection reached,"

in keeping his word at the sacrifice of his life, he acquired the perfection of truth in its highest degree.

Likewise in the Mūgapakkha Birth-Story, where he said, —

266. "'T is not that I my parents hate,
'T is not that glory I detest,
But since omniscience I held dear,
Therefore I kept my firm resolve,"

in resolving on a course of conduct that cost him his life, he acquired the perfection of resolution in its highest degree.

Likewise in the Ekarāja Birth-Story, where he said, —

267. "No fear has any one of me,
Nor have I fear of any one,
In my good-will to all I trust,
And love to dwell in lonely woods,"

in the exercise of feelings of good-will, and in taking no thought for his life, he acquired the perfection of good-will in its highest degree.

Likewise in the Lomahaṁsa Birth-Story, where he said,—

268. "I laid me down among the dead,
A pillow of their bones I made;
While from the villages around,
Some came to mock, and some to praise,"

while village children flocked about him, and some spat and others showered fragrant garlands upon him, he was indifferent alike to pleasure and pain, and acquired the perfection of indifference in its highest degree.

The above is an abridgment, but the full account is given in the Cariyā-Piṭaka.

Having thus fulfilled all the perfections, he said, in his existence as Vessantara, —

269. "This earth, unconscious though she be,
And ignorant of joy or grief,
E'en she then felt alms' mighty power,
And shook and quaked full seven times."

And having thus caused the earth to quake by his mighty deeds of merit, at the end of that existence he died, and was reborn in the Tusita heaven.

Accordingly the period from the time when he fell at the feet of Dīpaṁkara to his birth in the city of the Tusita gods constitutes the Distant Epoch.

---

§ 4. THE BIRTH OF THE BUDDHA.

Translated from the Introduction to the Jātaka (i.47[21]).

Now while the Future Buddha was still dwelling in the city of the Tusita gods, the "Buddha-Uproar," as it is called, took place. For there are three uproars which take place in the world, — the Cyclic-Uproar, the Buddha-Uproar, and the Universal-Monarch-Uproar. They occur as follows: —

When it is known that after the lapse of a hundred thousand years the cycle is to be renewed, the gods called Loka-byūhas, inhabitants of a heaven of sensual pleasure, wander about through the world, with hair let down and flying in the wind, weeping and wiping away their tears with their hands, and with their clothes red and in great disorder. And thus they make announcement: —

"Sirs, after the lapse of a hundred thousand years, the cycle is to be renewed; this world will be destroyed; also the mighty ocean will dry up; and this broad earth, and Sineru, the monarch of the mountains, will be burnt up and destroyed,—up to the Brahma heavens will the destruction of the world extend. Therefore, sirs, cultivate friendliness; cultivate compassion, joy, and indifference; wait on your mothers; wait on your fathers; and honor your elders among your kinsfolk."

This is called the Cyclic-Uproar.

Again, when it is known that after a lapse of a thousand years an omniscient Buddha is to arise in the world, the guardian angels of the world wander about, proclaiming:

"Sirs, after the lapse of a thousand years a Buddha will arise in the world."

This is called the Buddha-Uproar.

And lastly, when they realize that after the lapse of a hundred years a Universal Monarch is to arise, the terrestrial deities wander about, proclaiming:—

"Sirs, after the lapse of a hundred years a Universal Monarch is to arise in the world."

This is called the Universal-Monarch-Uproar. And these three are mighty uproars.

When of these three Uproars they hear the sound of the Buddha-Uproar, the gods of all ten thousand worlds come together into one place, and having ascertained what particular being is to be The Buddha, they approach him, and beseech him to become one. But it is not till after omens have appeared that they beseech him.

At that time, therefore, having all come together in one world, with the Cātum-Mahārājas, and with the Sakka, the Suyāma, the Santusita, the Paranimmita-Vasavatti, and the Mahā-Brahma of each several world, they approached the Future Buddha in the Tusita heaven, and besought him, saying,—

"Sir, it was not to acquire the glory of a Sakka, or of a Māra, or of a Brahma, or of a Universal Monarch, that you fulfilled the Ten Perfections; but it was to gain omniscience in order to save the world, that you fulfilled them. Sir, the time and fit season for your Buddhaship has now arrived."

But the Great Being, before assenting to their wish, made what is called the five great observations. He observed, namely, the time, the continent, the country, the family, and the mother and her span of life.

In the first of these observations he asked himself whether it was the right time or no. Now it is not the right time when the length of men's lives is more than a hundred thousand years. And why is it not the right time? Because mortals then forget about birth, old age, and death. And if The Buddhas, who always include in their teachings the Three Characteristics, were to attempt at such a time to discourse concerning transitoriness, misery, and the lack of substantive reality, men would not think it worth while listening to them, nor would they give them credence. Thus there would be no conversions made; and if there were no conversions, the dispensation would not conduce to salvation. This, therefore, is not the right time.

Also it is not the right time when men's lives are less than a hundred years. And why is it not the right time? Because mortals are then exceedingly corrupt; and an exhortation given to the exceedingly corrupt makes no impression, but, like a mark drawn with a stick on the surface of the water, it immediately disappears. This, therefore, also is not the right time.

But when the length of men's lives is between a hundred years and a hundred thousand years, then is it the right time. Now at that time men's lives were a hundred years; accordingly the Great Being observed that it was the right time for his birth.

Next he made the observation concerning the continent. Looking over the four continents with their attendant isles, he reflected: "In three of the continents the Buddhas are never born; only in the continent of India are they born." Thus he decided on the continent.

Next he made the observation concerning the place. "The continent of India is large," thought he, "being ten thousand leagues around. In which of its countries are The Buddhas born?" Thus he decided on the Middle Country.

The Middle Country is the country defined in the Vinaya as follows:—

"It lies in the middle, on this side of the town Kajaṅgala on the east, beyond which is Mahā-Sāla, and beyond that the border districts. It lies in the middle, on this side of the river Salalavatī on the southeast, beyond which are the border districts. It lies in the middle, on this side of the town Setakaṇṇika on the south, beyond which are the border districts. It lies in the middle, on this side of the Brahmanical town Thūṇa on the west, beyond which are the border districts. It lies in the middle, on this side of the hill Usīraddhaja on the north, beyond which are the border districts."

It is three hundred leagues in length, two hundred and fifty in breadth, and nine hundred in circumference. In this country are born The Buddhas, the Private Buddhas,[1] the Chief Disciples, the Eighty Great Disciples, the Universal Monarch, and other eminent ones, magnates of the warrior caste, of the Brahman caste, and the wealthy householders. "And in it is this city called Kapilavatthu," thought he, and concluded that there he ought to be born.

Then he made the observation concerning the family. "The Buddhas," thought he, "are never born into a family of the peasant caste, or of the servile caste; but into one of the warrior caste, or of the Brahman caste, whichever at the time is the higher in public estimation. The warrior caste is now the higher in public estimation. I will be born into a warrior family, and king Suddhodana shall be my father." Thus he decided on the family.

Then he made the observation concerning the mother. "The mother of a Buddha," thought he, "is never a wanton, nor a drunkard, but is one who has fulfilled the perfections through a hundred thousand cycles, and has kept the five precepts unbroken from the day of her birth. Now this queen Mahā-Māyā is such a one; and she shall be my mother."—

[1] See index, s. v.

"But what shall be her span of life?"[1] continued he. And he perceived that it was to be ten months and seven days.

Having thus made the five great observations, he kindly made the gods the required promise, saying, —

"Sirs, you are right. The time has come for my Buddhaship."

Then, surrounded by the gods of the Tusita heaven, and dismissing all the other gods, he entered the Nandana Grove of the Tusita capital, — for in each of the heavens there is a Nandana Grove. And here the gods said, "Attain in your next existence your high destiny," and kept reminding him that he had already paved the way to it by his accumulated merit. Now it was while he was thus dwelling, surrounded by these deities, and continually reminded of his accumulated merit, that he died, and was conceived in the womb of queen Mahā-Māyā. And in order that this matter may be fully understood, I will give the whole account in due order.

It is related that at that time the Midsummer Festival had been proclaimed in the city of Kapilavatthu, and the multitude were enjoying the feast. And queen Mahā-Māyā, abstaining from strong drink, and brilliant with garlands and perfumes, took part in the festivities for the six days previous to the day of full moon. And when it came to be the day of full moon, she rose early, bathed in perfumed water, and dispensed four hundred thousand pieces of money in great largess. And decked in full gala attire, she ate of the choicest food; after which she took the eight vows, and entered her elegantly furnished chamber of state. And lying down on the royal couch, she fell asleep and dreamed the following dream: —

The four guardian angels came and lifted her up, together with her couch, and took her away to the Himalaya Mountains. There, in the Manosilā table-land, which is sixty leagues in extent, they laid her under a prodigious sal-tree,

---

1 That is, "How long is she to live after conceiving me?" And the answer is, "Ten lunar [that is, the nine calendar] months of my mother's pregnancy, and seven days after my birth."

seven leagues in height, and took up their positions respectfully at one side. Then came the wives of these guardian angels, and conducted her to Anotatta Lake, and bathed her, to remove every human stain. And after clothing her with divine garments, they anointed her with perfumes and decked her with divine flowers. Not far off was Silver Hill, and in it a golden mansion. There they spread a divine couch with its head towards the east, and laid her down upon it. Now the Future Buddha had become a superb white elephant, and was wandering about at no great distance, on Gold Hill. Descending thence, he ascended Silver Hill, and approaching from the north, he plucked a white lotus with his silvery trunk, and trumpeting loudly, went into the golden mansion. And three times he walked round his mother's couch, with his right side towards it, and striking her on her right side, he seemed to enter her womb. Thus the conception took place in the Midsummer Festival.

On the next day the queen awoke, and told the dream to the king. And the king caused sixty-four eminent Brahmans to be summoned, and spread costly seats for them on ground festively prepared with green leaves, Dalbergia flowers, and so forth. The Brahmans being seated, he filled gold and silver dishes with the best of milk-porridge compounded with ghee, honey, and treacle; and covering these dishes with others, made likewise of gold and silver, he gave the Brahmans to eat. And not only with food, but with other gifts, such as new garments, tawny cows, and so forth, he satisfied them completely. And when their every desire had been satisfied, he told them the dream and asked them what would come of it.

"Be not anxious, great king!" said the Brahmans; "a child has planted itself in the womb of your queen, and it is a male child and not a female. You will have a son. And he, if he continue to live the household life, will become a Universal Monarch; but if he leave the household life and retire from the world, he will become a Buddha, and roll back the clouds of sin and folly of this world."

Now the instant the Future Buddha was conceived in the

womb of his mother, all the ten thousand worlds suddenly quaked, quivered, and shook. And the Thirty-two Prognostics appeared, as follows: an immeasurable light spread through ten thousand worlds; the blind recovered their sight, as if from desire to see this his glory; the deaf received their hearing; the dumb talked; the hunchbacked became straight of body; the lame recovered the power to walk; all those in bonds were freed from their bonds and chains; the fires went out in all the hells; the hunger and thirst of the Manes was stilled; wild animals lost their timidity; diseases ceased among men; all mortals became mild-spoken; horses neighed and elephants trumpeted in a manner sweet to the ear; all musical instruments gave forth their notes without being played upon; bracelets and other ornaments jingled; in all quarters of the heavens the weather became fair; a mild, cool breeze began to blow, very refreshing to men; rain fell out of season; water burst forth from the earth and flowed in streams; the birds ceased flying through the air; the rivers checked their flowing; in the mighty ocean the water became sweet; the ground became everywhere covered with lotuses of the five different colors; all flowers bloomed, both those on land and those that grow in the water; trunk-lotuses bloomed on the trunks of trees, branch-lotuses on the branches, and vine-lotuses on the vines; on the ground, stalk-lotuses, as they are called, burst through the overlying rocks and came up by sevens; in the sky were produced others, called hanging-lotuses; a shower of flowers fell all about; celestial music was heard to play in the sky; and the whole ten thousand worlds became one mass of garlands of the utmost possible magnificence, with waving chowries, and saturated with the incense-like fragrance of flowers, and resembled a bouquet of flowers sent whirling through the air, or a closely woven wreath, or a superbly decorated altar of flowers.

From the time the Future Buddha was thus conceived, four angels with swords in their hands kept guard, to ward off all harm from both the Future Buddha and the Future Buddha's mother. No lustful thought sprang up in the mind of the Future Buddha's mother; having reached the pinnacle of good fortune and of glory, she felt comfortable and well, and experienced no exhaustion of body. And within her womb she could distinguish the Future Buddha, like a white thread passed through a transparent jewel. And whereas a womb that has been occupied by a Future Buddha is like the shrine of a temple, and can never be occupied or used again, therefore it was that the mother of the Future Buddha died when he was seven days old, and was reborn in the Tusita heaven.

Now other women sometimes fall short of and sometimes run over the term of ten lunar months, and then bring forth either sitting or lying down; but not so the mother of a Future Buddha. She carries the Future Buddha in her womb for just ten months, and then brings forth while standing up. This is a characteristic of the mother of a Future Buddha. So also queen Mahā-Māyā carried the Future Buddha in her womb, as it were oil in a vessel, for ten months; and being then far gone with child, she grew desirous of going home to her relatives, and said to king Suddhodana, —

"Sire, I should like to visit my kinsfolk in their city Devadaha."

"So be it," said the king; and from Kapilavatthu to the city of Devadaha he had the road made even, and garnished it with plantain-trees set in pots, and with banners, and streamers; and, seating the queen in a golden palanquin borne by a thousand of his courtiers, he sent her away in great pomp.

Now between the two cities, and belonging to the inhabitants of both, there was a pleasure-grove of sal-trees, called Lumbini Grove. And at this particular time this grove was one mass of flowers from the ground to the topmost branches, while amongst the branches and flowers hummed swarms of bees of the five different colors, and flocks of various kinds of birds flew about warbling sweetly. Throughout the whole of Lumbini Grove the scene resembled the Cittalatā Grove in Indra's paradise, or the magnificently decorated banqueting pavilion of some potent king.

When the queen beheld it she became desirous of disporting herself therein, and the courtiers therefore took her into it. And going to the foot of the monarch sal-tree of the grove, she wished to take hold of one of its branches. And the sal-tree branch, like the tip of a well-steamed reed, bent itself down within reach of the queen's hand. Then she reached out her hand, and seized hold of the branch, and immediately her pains came upon her. Thereupon the people hung a curtain about her, and retired. So her delivery took place while she was standing up, and keeping fast hold of the sal-tree branch.

At that very moment came four pure-minded Mahā-Brahma angels bearing a golden net; and, receiving the Future Buddha on this golden net, they placed him before his mother and said, —

"Rejoice, O queen! A mighty son has been born to you."

Now other mortals on issuing from the maternal womb are smeared with disagreeable, impure matter; but not so the Future Buddha. He issued from his mother's womb like a preacher descending from his preaching-seat, or a man coming down a stair, stretching out both hands and both feet, unsmeared by any impurity from his mother's womb, and flashing pure and spotless, like a jewel thrown upon a vesture of Benares cloth. Notwithstanding this, for the sake of honoring the Future Buddha and his mother, there came two streams of water from the sky, and refreshed the Future Buddha and his mother.

Then the Brahma angels, after receiving him on their golden net, delivered him to the four guardian angels, who received him from their hands on a rug which was made of the skins of black antelopes, and was soft to the touch, being such as is used on state occasions; and the guardian angels delivered him to men who received him on a coil of fine cloth; and the men let him out of their hands on the ground, where he stood and faced the east. There, before him, lay many thousands of worlds, like a great open court; and in them, gods and men, making offerings to him of perfumes, garlands, and so on, were saying, —

"Great Being! There is none your equal, much less your superior."

When he had in this manner surveyed the four cardinal points, and the four intermediate ones, and the zenith, and the nadir, in short, all the ten directions in order, and had nowhere discovered his equal, he exclaimed, "This is the best direction," and strode forward seven paces, followed by Mahā-Brahma holding over him the white umbrella, Suyāma bearing the fan, and other divinities having the other symbols of royalty in their hands. Then, at the seventh stride, he halted, and with a noble voice, he shouted the shout of victory, beginning, —

"The chief am I in all the world."

Now in three of his existences did the Future Buddha utter words immediately on issuing from his mother's womb: namely, in his existence as Mahosadha; in his existence as Vessantara; and in this existence.

As respects his existence as Mahosadha, it is related that just as he was issuing from his mother's womb, Sakka, the king of the gods, came and placed in his hand some choice sandal-wood, and departed. And he closed his fist upon it, and issued forth.

"My child," said his mother, "what is it you bring with you in your hand?"

"Medicine, mother," said he.

Accordingly, as he was born with medicine in his hand, they gave him the name of Osadha-Dāraka [Medicine-Child]. Then they took the medicine, and placed it in an earthenware jar; and it was a sovereign remedy to heal all the blind, the deaf, and other afflicted persons who came to it. So the saying sprang up, "This is a great medicine, this is a great medicine!" And thus he received the name of Mahosadha [Great Medicine-Man].

Again, in the Vessantara existence, as he was issuing from his mother's womb, he stretched out his right hand, and said, —

"Pray, mother, is there anything in the house? I want to give alms."

Then, after he had completely issued forth, his mother said, —

"It 's a wealthy family, my son, into which you are born;" and putting his hand in her own, she had them place in his a purse containing a thousand pieces of money.

Lastly, in this birth he shouted the shout of victory abovementioned.

Thus in three of his existences did the Future Buddha utter words immediately on issuing from his mother's womb. And just as at the moment of his conception, so also at the moment of his birth appeared the Thirty-two Prognostics.

Now at the very time that our Future Buddha was born in Lumbini Grove there also came into existence the mother of Rāhula, and Channa the courtier, Kāḷudāyi the courtier, Kanthaka the king of horses, the Great Bo-tree, and the four urns full of treasure. Of these last, one was a quarter of a league in extent, another a half-league, the third three quarters of a league, and the fourth a league. These seven[1] are called the Connate Ones.

Then the inhabitants of both cities took the Future Buddha, and carried him to Kapilavatthu.

---

§ 5. THE YOUNG GOTAMID PRINCE.

Translated from the Introduction to the Jātaka (i.54[11]).

On this same day the happy and delighted hosts of the Heaven of the Thirty-three held a celebration, waving their cloaks and giving other signs of joy, because to king Suddhodana in Kapilavatthu had been born a son who should sit at the foot of the Bo-tree, and become a Buddha.

Now it came to pass at that time that an ascetic named Kāḷadevala, who was an intimate friend of king Suddhodana, and practised in the eight stages of meditation, went, after

[1] In making up this number the Future Buddha is to be counted as number 1, and the four urns of treasure together as number 7.

his daily meal, to the Heaven of the Thirty-three to take his noon-day rest. And as he was sitting there resting, he noticed these gods, and said,—

"Why do you frolic so joyously? Let me too know the reason."

"Sir," replied the gods, "it is because a son has been born to king Suddhodana, who shall sit at the foot of the Bo-tree, and become a Buddha, and cause the Wheel of the Doctrine to roll; in him we shall be permitted to behold the infinite and masterful ease of a Buddha, and shall hear the Doctrine."

On hearing this, the ascetic descended from the world of the gods in haste, and entered the dwelling of the king; and having seated himself on the seat assigned to him, he said,—

"Great king, I hear that a son has been born to you. I would see him."

Then the king had the prince magnificently dressed, and brought in, and carried up to do reverence to the ascetic. But the feet of the Future Buddha turned and planted themselves in the matted locks of the ascetic. For in that birth there was no one worthy of the Future Buddha's reverence; and if these ignorant people had succeeded in causing the Future Buddha to bow, the head of the ascetic would have split in seven pieces.

"It is not meet that I compass my own death," thought the ascetic, and rose from his seat, and with joined hands did reverence to the Future Buddha. And when the king had seen this wonder, he also did reverence to his son.

Now the ascetic could look backward into the past for forty world-cycles, and forward into the future for forty world-cycles,—in all, eighty world-cycles. And, noting on the person of the Future Buddha all the lucky marks and characteristics, he began to reflect and consider whether or not they prophesied his Buddhaship. And perceiving that undoubtedly he would become a Buddha, he thought to himself, "What a marvellous personage he is!" and smiled.

Next he considered in his mind whether he would live to see him attain the Buddhaship; and he perceived that he was not to have that opportunity. For he would die before that time, and be reborn in the formless mode of existence, where it would be out of the power of even a hundred or a thousand Buddhas to come and enlighten him. And he thought, "It will not be mine to behold this so marvellous a personage when he has become a Buddha. My loss, alas, will be great," and wept.

The people noticed his behavior, and said to him, —

"Our good father smiled but a moment ago, and now has begun to weep. Reverend sir, is any misfortune to happen to our young master?"

"No misfortune is to happen to him. He will become a Buddha without any manner of doubt."

"Then why did you weep?"

"I wept at the thought of my own great loss; for, alas, I am not to have an opportunity of seeing this marvellous person after he has become a Buddha."

Next he considered in his mind whether or not any of his relatives were to have the opportunity; and he saw that his sister's child Nālaka was to have it. And he went to his sister's house, and inquired, —

"Where is your son Nālaka?"

"Good father, he is in the house."

"Call him hither."

"My child," said he to the lad when he had come, "a son has been born in the family of Suddhodana the king, who is the coming Buddha. Thirty-five years from now he will become a Buddha, and you will have an opportunity of seeing him. Retire from the world this very day."

And the child did so, although he belonged to a family possessing eight hundred and seventy millions of treasure; for he thought, "My uncle would not lay such a command upon me for any trifling reason." Sending to the bazaar, he procured some yellow garments, and an earthenware bowl, and cut off his hair and his beard, and put on the yellow garments. And stretching out his joined hands in the direction of the Future Buddha, he said, "I retire from the world to follow earth's greatest being." Then he prostrated himself, so that he touched the ground with the fivefold contact. Having thus done reverence, he placed the bowl in his scrip, slung the latter over his shoulder, and going to the Himalaya Mountains, he there performed the duties of a monk.

And after the Great Being had achieved the absolute and supreme wisdom, Nālaka came to him, and had him prescribe the Nālaka course of conduct.[1] Then, returning to the Himalaya Mountains, he attained to saintship, and adopted that excellent course. And keeping alive for seven months more, and being at the time near a certain Gold Hill, he passed out of existence by that final extinction in which none of the elements of being remain.

Now on the fifth day they bathed the Future Buddha's head, saying, "We will perform the rite of choosing a name for him." And they prepared the royal palace by anointing it with four kinds of perfumes, and by scattering Dalbergia blossoms and other flowers, five sorts in all. And making some porridge of whole rice-grains boiled in milk, they invited one hundred and eight Brahmans, men who had mastered the three Vedas. And having seated these Brahmans in the royal palace, and fed them with delicate food, and showed them every attention, they asked them to observe the marks and characteristics of the Future Buddha's person, and to prophesy his fortune.

Among the hundred and eight,—

270. "Rāma, Dhaja, Lakkhaṇa, also Manti,
Koṇḍañña, Bhoja, Suyāma, Sudatta,
These Brahmans eight were there with senses six subdued;
They from the magic books disclosed his fortune."

These eight Brahmans were the fortune-tellers, being the same[2] who had interpreted the dream of the night of the

[1] The Nālaka course of conduct is given in the Nālaka Sutta of the Sutta-Nipāta, and consists of a number of precepts for leading the holy life.

[2] See p. 43. They presumably were the spokesmen for the sixty-four, as here for the one hundred and eight.

conception. Seven of these raised two fingers each, and gave a double interpretation, saying, "If a man possessing such marks and characteristics continue in the household life, he becomes a Universal Monarch; if he retire from the world, he becomes a Buddha." And then they set forth all the glory of a Universal Monarch.

But the youngest of them all, a youth whose clan-name was Koṇḍañña, after examining the splendid set of marks and characteristics on the person of the Future Buddha, raised only one finger, and gave but a single interpretation, saying, "There is here naught to make him stay in the household life. He will most undoubtedly become a Buddha, and remove the veil of ignorance and folly from the world." For this Koṇḍañña was one who had made an earnest wish under former Buddhas, and was now in his last existence. Therefore it was that he outstripped the other seven in knowledge, and saw but one future; inasmuch as a person possessed of such marks and characteristics would never stay in the household life, but would undoubtedly become a Buddha. So he raised only one finger, and gave that interpretation.

Then the seven Brahmans went home and said to their sons, "Children, we are old, but whether we ourselves are alive or not when the son of Suddhodana the king shall attain omniscience, you, at least, should then retire from the world under his dispensation."

And after these seven persons had lived out their term of life they passed away according to their deeds; but Koṇḍañña, being younger, was still alive and hale. And when the Great Being, after making the great retirement in pursuit of wisdom, had arrived at Uruvelā in his progress from place to place, he thought: "How pleasant indeed is this spot! How suitable for the struggles of a young man desirous of struggling!" and took up his abode there. Koṇḍañña heard the news that the Great Being had retired from the world, and drawing near to the sons of those seven Brahmans, he spoke to them as follows:—

"I hear that prince Siddhattha has retired from the world. Now he will unquestionably become a Buddha, and if your fathers were alive they would follow after him this very day. If you also would like to retire from the world, come with me. I mean to follow after that man in his retirement from the world."

But they could not all agree; and three of them did not retire from the world. But the remaining four did so, and made the Brahman Koṇḍañña their chief. And these five persons became known as the "Band of Five Elders."

Then said the king, "What shall my son see to make him retire from the world?"

"The four signs."

"What four?"

"A decrepit old man, a diseased man, a dead man, and a monk."

"From this time forth," said the king, "let no such persons be allowed to come near my son. It will never do for my son to become a Buddha. What I would wish to see is my son exercising sovereign rule and authority over the four great continents and the two thousand attendant isles, and walking through the heavens surrounded by a retinue thirty-six leagues in circumference." And when he had so spoken he placed guards for a distance of a quarter of a league in each of the four directions, in order that none of these four kinds of men might come within sight of his son.

On this same day, also, eighty thousand clansmen assembled together in the festival-hall, and each dedicated a son, saying, —

"Whether the young prince become a Buddha or a king, we will each one give a son: so that if he become a Buddha, he shall be followed and surrounded by monks of the warrior caste; and if he become a king, by nobles of the warrior caste."

And the king procured nurses for the Future Buddha, — women of fine figure, and free from all blemish. And so the Future Buddha began to grow, surrounded by an immense retinue, and in great splendor.

Now on a certain day the king celebrated the Sowing

Festival, as it was called. On that day they used to decorate the whole city, so that it looked like a palace of the gods; and all the slaves and other servants would put on new tunics; and, perfumed and garlanded, they would assemble together at the king's palace, where a thousand plows were yoked for the royal plowing.

On this occasion there were one hundred and eight plows, all save one ornamented with silver, as were also the reins for the oxen and the cross-bars of the plows. But the plow that was held by the king was ornamented with red gold, as also the horns, the reins, and the goads for the oxen. And the king issued forth with a large retinue, taking his son along with him. And in the field where the plowing was to be done was a solitary rose-apple tree of thick foliage and dense shade. Underneath this tree the king had a couch placed for the young prince, and spread over his head a canopy that was studded with gold stars; and he surrounded him with a screen, and appointed those that should watch by him; and then, decked with all his ornaments and surrounded by his courtiers, he proceeded to the place where they were to plow. On arriving there, the king took the gold plow, and the courtiers took the silver plows,— one hundred and eight save one, and the farmers the other plows; and then all plowed forward and back. The king went from the hither side to the farther side, and from the farther side back again; and the pomp and magnificence of the festival was at its climax.

Now the nurses who were sitting about the Future Buddha came out from behind the screen to behold the royal magnificence. And the Future Buddha, looking hither and thither and seeing no one, arose in haste and sat him down cross-legged, and mastering his inspirations and his expirations, entered on the first trance. The nurses delayed a little, being detained by the abundance of good things to eat. And the shadows of the other trees passed over to the east, but the shadow of the rose-apple tree remained steadily circular. Suddenly the nurses remembered that they had left their young master alone; and raising the screen, they entered and saw the Future Buddha sitting cross-legged on the couch, and also noticed the miracle of the shadow. Then they went and announced to the king, —

"Sire, thus and so is the prince sitting; and the shadows of the other trees have passed over to the east, but the shadow of the rose-apple tree remains steadily circular."

And the king came in haste, and seeing the miracle, he did obeisance to his son, saying, "This, dear child, is my second obeisance."

And thus, in due course, the Future Buddha attained to the age of sixteen years. And the king built three palaces for the Future Buddha, suited to the three seasons, — one of nine stories, another of seven stories, and another of five stories. And he provided him with forty thousand dancing girls. And the Future Buddha, with his gayly dressed dancers, was like a god surrounded by hosts of houris; and attended by musical instruments that sounded of themselves, and in the enjoyment of great magnificence, he lived, as the seasons changed, in each of these three palaces. And the mother of Rāhula was his principal queen.

Now while he was thus enjoying great splendor, one day there arose the following discussion among his relatives: —

"Siddhattha is wholly given over to pleasure, and is not training himself in any manly art. What could he do if war were to occur?"

The king sent for the Future Buddha, and said, —

"My child, your relatives are saying that you are not training yourself, but are wholly given over to pleasure. Now what do you think we had best do?"

"Sire, I do not need to train myself. Let the crier go about the city beating the drum, to announce that I will show my proficiency. On the seventh day from now I will show my proficiency to my relatives."

The king did so. And the Future Buddha assembled together bowmen that could shoot like lightning and at a hair's-breadth; and in the midst of the populace, and before his kinsfolk, he exhibited a twelvefold skill, such as none of the other bowmen could equal. All of which is to be understood after the manner related in the Sarabhañga Birth-Story. So the assembly of his kinsfolk doubted him no longer.

---

§ 6. THE GREAT RETIREMENT.

Translated from the Introduction to the Jātaka (i.58[31]).

Now on a certain day the Future Buddha wished to go to the park, and told his charioteer to make ready the chariot. Accordingly the man brought out a sumptuous and elegant chariot, and adorning it richly, he harnessed to it four state-horses of the Sindhava breed, as white as the petals of the white lotus, and announced to the Future Buddha that everything was ready. And the Future Buddha mounted the chariot, which was like to a palace of the gods, and proceeded towards the park.

"The time for the enlightenment of prince Siddhattha draweth nigh," thought the gods; "we must show him a sign:" and they changed one of their number into a decrepit old man, broken-toothed, gray-haired, crooked and bent of body, leaning on a staff, and trembling, and showed him to the Future Buddha, but so that only he and the charioteer saw him.

Then said the Future Buddha to the charioteer, in the manner related in the Mahāpadāna,—

"Friend, pray, who is this man? Even his hair is not like that of other men." And when he heard the answer, he said, "Shame on birth, since to every one that is born old age must come." And agitated in heart, he thereupon returned and ascended his palace.

"Why has my son returned so quickly?" asked the king.

"Sire, he has seen an old man," was the reply; "and

because he has seen an old man, he is about to retire from the world."

"Do you want to kill me, that you say such things? Quickly get ready some plays to be performed before my son. If we can but get him to enjoying pleasure, he will cease to think of retiring from the world." Then the king extended the guard to half a league in each direction.

Again, on a certain day, as the Future Buddha was going to the park, he saw a diseased man whom the gods had fashioned; and having again made inquiry, he returned, agitated in heart, and ascended his palace.

And the king made the same inquiry and gave the same orders as before; and again extending the guard, placed them for three quarters of a league around.

And again on a certain day, as the Future Buddha was going to the park, he saw a dead man whom the gods had fashioned; and having again made inquiry, he returned, agitated in heart, and ascended his palace.

And the king made the same inquiry and gave the same orders as before; and again extending the guard, placed them for a league around.

And again on a certain day, as the Future Buddha was going to the park, he saw a monk, carefully and decently clad, whom the gods had fashioned; and he asked his charioteer, "Pray, who is this man?"

Now although there was no Buddha in the world, and the charioteer had no knowledge of either monks or their good qualities, yet by the power of the gods he was inspired to say, "Sire, this is one who has retired from the world;" and he thereupon proceeded to sound the praises of retirement from the world. The thought of retiring from the world was a pleasing one to the Future Buddha, and this day he went on until he came to the park. The repeaters of the Dīgha,[1] however, say that he went to the park after having seen all the Four Signs on one and the same day.

When he had disported himself there throughout the day,

[1] Dīgha-Nikāya: see General Introduction.

and had bathed in the royal pleasure-tank, he went at sunset and sat down on the royal resting-stone with the intention of adorning himself. Then gathered around him his attendants with diverse-colored cloths, many kinds and styles of ornaments, and with garlands, perfumes, and ointments. At that instant the throne on which Sakka was sitting grew hot. And Sakka, considering who it could be that was desirous of dislodging him, perceived that it was the time of the adornment of a Future Buddha. And addressing Vissakamma, he said,—

"My good Vissakamma, to-night, in the middle watch, prince Siddhattha will go forth on the Great Retirement, and this is his last adorning of himself. Go to the park, and adorn that eminent man with celestial ornaments."

"Very well," said Vissakamma, in assent; and came on the instant, by his superhuman power, into the presence of the Future Buddha. And assuming the guise of a barber, he took from the real barber the turban-cloth, and began to wind it round the Future Buddha's head; but as soon as the Future Buddha felt the touch of his hand, he knew that it was no man, but a god.

Now once round his head took up a thousand cloths, and the fold was like to a circlet of precious stones; the second time round took another thousand cloths, and so on, until ten times round had taken up ten thousand cloths. Now let no one think, "How was it possible to use so many cloths on one small head?" for the very largest of them all had only the size of a sāma-creeper blossom, and the others that of kutumbaka flowers. Thus the Future Buddha's head resembled a kuyyaka blossom twisted about with lotus filaments.

And having adorned himself with great richness,—while adepts in different kinds of tabors and tom-toms were showing their skill, and Brahmans with cries of victory and joy, and bards and poets with propitious words and shouts of praise saluted him,—he mounted his superbly decorated chariot.

At this juncture, Suddhodana the king, having heard that

the mother of Rāhula had brought forth a son, sent a messenger, saying, "Announce the glad news to my son."

On hearing the message, the Future Buddha said, "An impediment [rāhula] has been born; a fetter has been born."

"What did my son say?" questioned the king; and when he had heard the answer, he said, "My grandson's name shall be prince Rāhula from this very day."

But the Future Buddha in his splendid chariot entered the city with a pomp and magnificence of glory that enraptured all minds. At the same moment Kisā Gotamī, a virgin of the warrior caste, ascended to the roof of her palace, and beheld the beauty and majesty of the Future Buddha, as he circumambulated the city; and in her pleasure and satisfaction at the sight, she burst forth into this song of joy:—

271. "Full happy now that mother is,
Full happy now that father is,
Full happy now that woman is,
Who owns this lord so glorious!"

On hearing this, the Future Buddha thought, "In beholding a handsome figure the heart of a mother attains Nirvana, the heart of a father attains Nirvana, the heart of a wife attains Nirvana. This is what she says. But wherein does Nirvana consist?" And to him, whose mind was already averse to passion, the answer came: "When the fire of lust is extinct, that is Nirvana; when the fires of hatred and infatuation are extinct, that is Nirvana; when pride, false belief, and all other passions and torments are extinct, that is Nirvana. She has taught me a good lesson. Certainly, Nirvana is what I am looking for. It behooves me this very day to quit the household life, and to retire from the world in quest of Nirvana.[1] I will send this lady a teacher's fee." And

[1] The Future Buddha puns upon the word "happy" in Kisā Gotamī's verses. The word in Pāli is *nibbuta*, and is in form a past passive participle of a verb which perhaps does not occur in Pāli in any finite form, but which appears in Sanskrit as *nirvr*. Now there is a Pāli verb of which the third person singular present indicative is *nibbāyati*, and from this

loosening from his neck a pearl necklace worth a hundred thousand pieces of money, he sent it to Kisā Gotamī. And great was her satisfaction at this, for she thought, "Prince Siddhattha has fallen in love with me, and has sent me a present."

And the Future Buddha entered his palace in great splendor, and lay on his couch of state. And straightway richly dressed women, skilled in all manner of dance and song, and beautiful as celestial nymphs, gathered about him with all kinds of musical instruments, and with dance, song, and music they endeavored to please him. But the Future Buddha's aversion to passion did not allow him to take pleasure in the spectacle, and he fell into a brief slumber. And the women, exclaiming, "He for whose sake we should perform has fallen asleep. Of what use is it to weary ourselves any longer?" threw their various instruments on the ground, and lay down. And the lamps fed with sweet-smelling oil continued to burn. And the Future Buddha awoke, and seating himself cross-legged on his couch, perceived these women lying asleep, with their musical instruments scattered about them on the floor, — some with their bodies wet with trickling phlegm and spittle; some grinding their teeth, and muttering and talking in their sleep; some with their mouths open; and some with their dress fallen apart so as plainly to

---

verb is formed the verbal noun *nibbāna* (Sanskrit, *Nirvāṇa*). *Nibbuta* is constantly made to do duty as past passive participle to this verb, so that what would be the true form (*nibbāta*) is never found. The Future Buddha therefore puns when he pretends that Kisā Gotamī was using *nibbuta* as the participle of *nibbāyati*, and was urging him to Nirvana.

The verb *nibbāyati* means "to be extinguished," as the flame of a candle; and, when used as a metaphysical term, refers to the fires of lust, desire, etc. And as when fire is extinguished coolness results (a consummation devoutly to be wished in a hot climate like India), the verb acquires the further meaning of "be assuaged," "become happy." And in like manner the verbal noun Nirvana (in Pāli *nibbāna*), meaning both literally and metaphorically "becoming extinguished," comes to stand for the *summum bonum*.

I add a retranslation of the passage, to show the punning meanings given by the Future Buddha to the words, *nibbuta*, *nibbāyati*, and Nirvana: —

disclose their loathsome nakedness. This great alteration in their appearance still further increased his aversion for sensual pleasures. To him that magnificent apartment, as splendid as the palace of Sakka, began to seem like a cemetery filled with dead bodies impaled and left to rot; and the three modes of existence appeared like houses all ablaze. And breathing forth the solemn utterance, "How oppressive and stifling is it all!" his mind turned ardently to retiring from the world. "It behooves me to go forth on the Great Retirement this very day," said he; and he arose from his couch, and coming near the door, called out, —

"Who's there?"

"Master, it is I, Channa," replied the courtier who had been sleeping with his head on the threshold.[1]

"I wish to go forth on the Great Retirement to-day. Saddle a horse for me."

"Yes, sire." And taking saddle and bridle with him, the courtier started for the stable. There, by the light of lamps fed with sweet-smelling oils, he perceived the mighty steed Kanthaka in his pleasant quarters, under a canopy of cloth beautified with a pattern of jasmine flowers. "This is the

---

"Nirvana hath that mother gained,
Nirvana hath that father gained,
Nirvana hath that woman gained,
Who owns this lord so glorious!"

On hearing this, the Future Buddha thought, "In beholding a handsome form the heart of a mother is made happy (*nibbāyati*), the heart of a father is made happy, the heart of a wife is made happy. This is what she says. But wherein does happiness (*nibbuta*) consist?" And to him whose mind was already averse to passion, the answer came: "When the fire of lust is assuaged (*nibbuta*), that is happiness (*nibbuta*); when the fires of hatred and infatuation are assuaged, that is happiness; when pride, false belief, and all other passions and torments are assuaged, that is happiness. She has taught me a good lesson. Certainly, happiness (Nirvana) is what I am looking for. It behooves me this very day to quit the household life and to retire from the world in quest of happiness. I will send this lady a teacher's fee."

[1] In India it is customary to hang doors at the height of about two feet from the ground for the sake of coolness and ventilation. The threshold is thus exposed even when the door is shut.

one for me to saddle to-day," thought he; and he saddled Kanthaka.

"He is drawing the girth very tight," thought Kanthaka, whilst he was being saddled; "it is not at all as on other days, when I am saddled for rides in the park and the like. It must be that to-day my master wishes to issue forth on the Great Retirement." And in his delight he neighed a loud neigh. And that neigh would have spread through the whole town, had not the gods stopped the sound, and suffered no one to hear it.

Now the Future Buddha, after he had sent Channa on his errand, thought to himself, "I will take just one look at my son;" and, rising from the couch on which he was sitting, he went to the suite of apartments occupied by the mother of Rāhula, and opened the door of her chamber. Within the chamber was burning a lamp fed with sweet-smelling oil, and the mother of Rāhula lay sleeping on a couch strewn deep with jasmine and other flowers, her hand resting on the head of her son. When the Future Buddha reached the threshold, he paused, and gazed at the two from where he stood.

"If I were to raise my wife's hand from off the child's head, and take him up, she would awake, and thus prevent my departure. I will first become a Buddha, and then come back and see my son." So saying, he descended from the palace.

Now that which is said in the Jātaka Commentary, "At that time Rāhula was seven days old," is not found in the other commentaries. Therefore the account above given is to be accepted.

When the Future Buddha had thus descended from the palace, he came near to his horse, and said,—

"My dear Kanthaka, save me now this one night; and then, when thanks to you I have become a Buddha, I will save the world of gods and men." And thereupon he vaulted upon Kanthaka's back.

Now Kanthaka was eighteen cubits long from his neck to his tail, and of corresponding height; he was strong and swift, and white all over like a polished conch-shell. If he neighed or stamped, the sound was so loud as to spread through the whole city; therefore the gods exerted their power, and muffled the sound of his neighing, so that no one heard it; and at every step he took they placed the palms of their hands under his feet.

The Future Buddha rode on the mighty back of the mighty steed, made Channa hold on by the tail, and so arrived at midnight at the great gate of the city.

Now the king, in order that the Future Buddha should not at any time go out of the city without his knowledge, had caused each of the two leaves of the gate to be made so heavy as to need a thousand men to move it. But the Future Buddha had a vigor and a strength that was equal, when reckoned in elephant-power, to the strength of ten thousand million elephants, and, reckoned in man-power, to the strength of a hundred thousand million men.

"If," thought he, "the gate does not open, I will straightway grip tight hold of Kanthaka with my thighs, and, seated as I am on Kanthaka's back, and with Channa holding on by the tail, I will leap up and carry them both with me over the wall, although its height be eighteen cubits."

"If," thought Channa, "the gate is not opened, I will place my master on my shoulder, and tucking Kanthaka under my arm by passing my right hand round him and under his belly, I will leap up and carry them both with me over the wall."

"If," thought Kanthaka, "the gate is not opened, with my master seated as he is on my back, and with Channa holding on by my tail, I will leap up and carry them both with me over the wall."

Now if the gate had not opened, verily one or another of these three persons would have accomplished that whereof he thought; but the divinity that inhabited the gate opened it for them.

At this moment came Māra,[1] with the intention of per-

[1] The Buddhists recognize no real devil. Māra, the ruler of the sixth and highest heaven of sensual pleasure, approaches the nearest to our Satan. He stands for the pleasures of sense, and hence is The Buddha's natural enemy.

suading the Future Buddha to turn back; and standing in the air, he said, —

"Sir, go not forth! For on the seventh day from now the wheel of empire will appear to you, and you shall rule over the four great continents and their two thousand attendant isles. Sir, turn back!"

"Who are you?"

"I am Vasavatti."

"Māra, I knew that the wheel of empire was on the point of appearing to me; but I do not wish for sovereignty. I am about to cause the ten thousand worlds to thunder with my becoming a Buddha."

"I shall catch you," thought Māra, "the very first time you have a lustful, malicious, or unkind thought." And, like an ever-present shadow, he followed after, ever on the watch for some slip.

Thus the Future Buddha, casting away with indifference a universal sovereignty already in his grasp, — spewing it out as if it were but phlegm, — departed from the city in great splendor on the full-moon day of the month Āsāḷhī,[1] when the moon was in Libra. And when he had gone out from the city, he became desirous of looking back at it; but no sooner had the thought arisen in his mind, than the broad earth, seeming to fear lest the Great Being might neglect to perform the act of looking back, split and turned round like a potter's wheel.[2] When the Future Buddha had stood a while facing the city and gazing upon it, and had indicated in that place the spot for the "Shrine of the Turning Back of Kanthaka," he turned Kanthaka in the direction in which he meant to go, and proceeded on his way in great honor and exceeding glory.

For they say the deities bore sixty thousand torches in front of him, and sixty thousand behind him, and sixty

---

[1] About the first of July.

[2] I think the conception here is that a round portion of the earth, on which the Future Buddha stood, turned around like a modern railroad turn-table, thus detaching itself from the rest and turning the Future Buddha with it.

thousand on the right hand, and sixty thousand on the left hand. Other deities, standing on the rim of the world, bore torches past all numbering; and still other deities, as well as serpents and birds, accompanied him, and did him homage with heavenly perfumes, garlands, sandal-wood powder, and incense. And the sky was as full of coral flowers as it is of pouring water at the height of the rainy season. Celestial choruses were heard; and on every side bands of music played, some of eight instruments, and some of sixty, — sixty-eight hundred thousand instruments in all. It was as when the storm-clouds thunder on the sea, or when the ocean roars against the Yugandhara rocks.

Advancing in this glory, the Future Buddha in one night passed through three kingdoms, and at the end of thirty leagues he came to the river named Anomā.

But was this as far as the horse could go? Certainly not. For he was able to travel round the world from end to end, as it were round the rim of a wheel lying on its hub, and yet get back before breakfast and eat the food prepared for him. But on this occasion the fragrant garlands and other offerings which the gods and the serpents and the birds threw down upon him from the sky buried him up to his haunches; and as he was obliged to drag his body and cut his way through the tangled mass, he was greatly delayed. Hence it was that he went only thirty leagues.

And the Future Buddha, stopping on the river-bank, said to Channa, —

"What is the name of this river?"

"Sire, its name is Anomā [Illustrious]."

"And my retirement from the world shall also be called Anomā," replied the Future Buddha. Saying this, he gave the signal to his horse with his heel; and the horse sprang over the river, which had a breadth of eight usabhas,[1] and landed on the opposite bank. And the Future Buddha, dismounting and standing on the sandy beach that stretched away like a sheet of silver, said to Channa, —

---

1 An usabha is 140 cubits.

"My good Channa, take these ornaments and Kanthaka and go home. I am about to retire from the world."

"Sire, I also will retire from the world."

Three times the Future Buddha refused him, saying, "It is not for you to retire from the world. Go now!" and made him take the ornaments and Kanthaka.

Next he thought, "These locks of mine are not suited to a monk; but there is no one fit to cut the hair of a Future Buddha. Therefore I will cut them off myself with my sword." And grasping a simitar with his right hand, he seized his top-knot with his left hand, and cut it off, together with the diadem. His hair thus became two finger-breadths in length, and curling to the right, lay close to his head. As long as he lived it remained of that length, and the beard was proportionate. And never again did he have to cut either hair or beard.

Then the Future Buddha seized hold of his top-knot and diadem, and threw them into the air, saying,—

"If I am to become a Buddha, let them stay in the sky; but if not, let them fall to the ground."

The top-knot and jewelled turban mounted for a distance of a league into the air, and there came to a stop. And Sakka, the king of the gods, perceiving them with his divine eye, received them in an appropriate jewelled casket, and established it in the Heaven of the Thirty-three as the "Shrine of the Diadem."

272. "His hair he cut, so sweet with many pleasant scents,
This Chief of Men, and high impelled it towards the sky;
And there god Vāsava, the god with thousand eyes,
In golden casket caught it, bowing low his head."

Again the Future Buddha thought, "These garments of mine, made of Benares cloth, are not suited to a monk."

Now the Mahā-Brahma god, Ghaṭīkāra, who had been a friend of his in the time of the Buddha Kassapa, and whose affection for him had not grown old in the long interval since that Buddha, thought to himself,—

"To-day my friend has gone forth on the Great Retirement. I will bring him the requisites of a monk."

273. "Robes, three in all, the bowl for alms,
The razor, needle, and the belt,
And water-strainer, — just these eight
Are needed by th' ecstatic monk."

Taking the above eight requisites of a monk, he gave them to him.

When the Future Buddha had put on this most excellent vesture, the symbol of saintship and of retirement from the world, he dismissed Channa, saying, —

"Channa, go tell my father and my mother from me that I am well."

And Channa did obeisance to the Future Buddha; and keeping his right side towards him, he departed.

But Kanthaka, who had stood listening to the Future Buddha while he was conferring with Channa, was unable to bear his grief at the thought, "I shall never see my master any more." And as he passed out of sight, his heart burst, and he died, and was reborn in the Heaven of the Thirty-three as the god Kanthaka.

At first the grief of Channa had been but single; but now he was oppressed with a second sorrow in the death of Kanthaka, and came weeping and wailing to the city.

§ 7. THE GREAT STRUGGLE.

Translated from the Introduction to the Jātaka (i.65[29]).

Now the Future Buddha, having thus retired from the world, — in that place there was a mango-grove named Anupiya, and here he first spent a week in the joy of having retired from the world, — in one day went on foot to Rājagaha, a distance of thirty leagues, and entering the city, he begged for food from house to house without passing any by. By the beauty of the Future Buddha, the whole city was thrown into a commotion, like that into which Rājagaha was thrown by the entrance of Dhanapālaka, or like that into which the heavenly city was thrown by the entrance of the chief of the Titans.

Then ran the king's men to the palace, and made announcement, —

"Sire, there is a being of such and such appearance going about the city begging for food. Whether he be a god, or a man, or a serpent, or a bird, we do not know."

Then the king, standing on the roof of his palace, and thence beholding the Great Being, became amazed and astonished, and commanded his men, —

"Look ye now! Go and investigate this! If this person be not a man, he will vanish from sight as soon as he leaves the city; if, namely, he be a god, he will depart by way of the air; if a serpent, he will sink into the ground. But if he be a human being, he will eat the food he has obtained in alms."

Now the Great Being, after collecting a number of scraps, sufficient, as he judged, for his sustenance, left the city by the same gate he had entered, and sitting down with his face to the east, in the shade of Paṇḍava rock, he attempted to eat his meal. But his stomach turned, and he felt as if his inwards were on the point of coming out by his mouth. Thereupon, in the midst of his distress at that repulsive food, — for in that existence he had never before so much as seen such fare, — he began to admonish himself, saying, "Siddhattha, although you were born into a family having plenty to eat and drink, into a station in life where you lived on fragrant third season's rice [1] with various sauces of the finest flavors, yet when you saw a monk clad in garments taken from the rubbish heap, you exclaimed, 'Oh, when shall I be like him, and eat food which I have begged? Will that time ever come?' And then you retired from the world. And

---

[1] A garment new, a new-built house,
A new umbrella, and a bride, —
The new is good; but long-kept rice
And long-kept servants men do praise.

From the Sanskrit of the *Nītipradīpa*, 15, as given by Böhtlingk, *Indische Sprüche*, 3410.

now that you have your wish, and have renounced all, what, pray, is this you are doing?" When he had thus admonished himself, his disgust subsided, and he ate his meal.

Then the king's men went and announced to the king what they had seen. And the king, on hearing the report of the messengers, issued hastily from the city, and approaching the Future Buddha, and being pleased with his deportment, he tendered him all his kingly glory.

"Great king," replied the Future Buddha, "I do not seek for the gratification of my senses or my passions, but have retired from the world for the sake of the supreme and absolute enlightenment."

"Verily," said the king, when his repeated offers had all been refused, "you are sure to become a Buddha; but when that happens, your first journey must be to my kingdom."

The above is an abridgment, but the full account, beginning with the lines,—

> "I sing the man of insight keen,
> And his retirement from the world,"

can be found by referring to the "Discourse on Retirement from the World," and its commentary.

Then the Future Buddha, having made the king the required promise, proceeded on his way; and coming to Āḷāra Kālāma and Uddaka, the disciple of Rāma, he acquired from them the eight stages of meditation. But becoming convinced that they did not lead to enlightenment,[1] he ceased to practise them. And being desirous of making the Great Struggle, so as to show the world of gods and men his fortitude and heroism, he went to Uruvelā, and saying, "Truly, delightful is this spot," he there took up his abode, and began the Great Struggle.

And those five persons, Koṇḍañña and the others,[2] who since their retirement from the world, were wandering about for alms through villages, market-towns, and royal cities, here met with the Future Buddha. And during the six

[1] See pages 334–8. [2] See pages 52–3.

years of the Great Struggle, they swept his cell, and did all manner of service for him, and kept constantly at his beck and call, all the time saying, "Now he will become a Buddha, now he will become a Buddha."

And the Future Buddha, thinking, "I will carry austerity to the uttermost," tried various plans, such as living on one sesamum seed or on one grain of rice a day, and even ceased taking nourishment altogether, and moreover rebuffed the gods when they came and attempted to infuse nourishment through the pores of his skin. By this lack of nourishment his body became emaciated to the last degree, and lost its golden color, and became black, and his thirty-two physical characteristics as a great being became obscured. Now, one day, as he was deep in a trance of suppressed breathing, he was attacked by violent pains, and fell senseless to the ground, at one end of his walking-place.

And certain of the deities said, "The monk Gotama is dead;" but others said, "This is a practice of the saints." Then those who thought he was dead went to king Suddhodana, and announced to him that his son was dead.

"Did he die after becoming a Buddha, or before?" asked the king.

"He was unable to become a Buddha, but in making the Struggle, he fell to the ground and died."

When the king heard this, he refused to credit it, saying, "I do not believe it. Death cannot come to my son before he attains to enlightenment."

But why would not the king believe it? Because of the miracles he had seen, — the first when the ascetic Kāḷadevala had been compelled to do homage to the Future Buddha, and the other which happened to the rose-apple tree.

But the Future Buddha recovering his consciousness, and standing up, the deities went a second time to the king, and told him that his son was well again.

Said the king, "I knew that my son could not have died."

Now the six years which the Great Being thus spent in austerities were like time spent in endeavoring to tie the air into knots. And coming to the decision, "These austerities are not the way to enlightenment," he went begging through villages and market-towns for ordinary material food, and lived upon it. And his thirty-two physical characteristics as a great being again appeared, and the color of his body became like unto gold.

Then the band of five priests thought, "It is now six years that this man has been performing austerities without being able to attain to omniscience. And how much less can he be expected to do so in future, now that he has again taken to ordinary material food begged from town to town! He has become luxurious, and given up the Struggle. For us to look for any benefit to come from that quarter would be as reasonable as if a man were to imagine he could bathe his head in a dew-drop. We will have nothing more to do with him." With that they took their bowls and robes, and left the Great Being, and going eighteen leagues off, entered Isipatana.

---

§ 8. THE ATTAINMENT OF BUDDHASHIP.

Translated from the Introduction to the Jātaka (i.68[8]).

Now at that time there lived in Uruvelā a girl named Sujātā, who had been born in the family of the householder Senāni, in General's Town. On reaching maturity she made a prayer to a certain banyan-tree, saying, "If I get a husband of equal rank with myself, and my first-born is a son, I will make a yearly offering to you of the value of a hundred thousand pieces of money." And her prayer had been successful.

And wishing to make her offering on the day of full moon of the month Visākhā, full six years after the Great Being commenced his austerities, she first pastured a thousand cows in Laṭṭhimadhu Wood, and fed their milk to five hundred cows, and the milk of these five hundred cows to two hundred and fifty, and so on down to feeding the milk of sixteen cows to eight. This "working the milk in and in," as it is called, was done to increase the thickness and the sweetness and the strength-giving properties of the milk. And when it came to be the full-moon day of Visākhā, she resolved to make her offering, and rose up early in the morning, just when night was breaking into day, and gave orders to milk the eight cows. The calves had not come at the teats of the cows; yet as soon as new pails were put under the udders, the milk flowed in streams of its own accord. When she saw this miracle, Sujātā took the milk with her own hands and placed it in a new vessel, and herself made a fire and began to cook it. While the milk-rice was cooking, immense bubbles arose, and turning to the right, went round together; but not a single drop ran over the edge, and not a particle of smoke went up from the fireplace. On this occasion the four guardian angels were present, and stood guard over the fireplace; Mahā-Brahma bore aloft the canopy of state, and Sakka raked the fire-brands together and made the fire blaze up brightly. And just as a man crushes honey out of a honey-comb that has formed around a stick, so the deities by their superhuman power collected an amount of vital sap sufficient for the sustenance of the gods and men of all the four great continents and their two thousand attendant isles, and infused it into the milk-rice. At other times, to be sure, the deities infuse this sap into each mouthful; but on the day of the attainment of the Buddhaship, and on the day of decease, they place it in the kettle itself.

When Sujātā had seen so many miracles appear to her in one day, she said to her slave-girl Puṇṇā, —

"Puṇṇā, dear girl, the deity is very graciously disposed to us to-day. I have never before seen so many marvellous things happen in so short a time. Run, quickly, and get everything ready at the holy place."

"Yes, my lady," replied the slave-girl, and ran in great haste to the foot of the tree.

Now that night the Future Buddha had five great dreams, and on considering their meaning reached the conclusion, "Without doubt I shall become a Buddha this very day."

And when night was over, and he had cared for his person, he came early in the morning to that tree, to await the hour to go begging. And when he sat down he illumined the whole tree with his radiance.

Then came Puṇṇā, and saw the Future Buddha sitting at the foot of the tree, contemplating the eastern quarter of the world. And when she beheld the radiance from his body lighting up the whole tree with a golden color, she became greatly excited, saying to herself, "Our deity, methinks, has come down from the tree to-day, and has seated himself, ready to receive our offering in person." And she ran in great haste, and told Sujātā of the matter.

When Sujātā heard this news, she was overjoyed; and saying, "From this day forth be to me in the room of an eldest daughter," she decked Puṇṇā with all the ornaments appropriate to that position. And since a Future Buddha on the day he attains the Buddhaship must needs receive a golden dish worth a hundred thousand pieces of money, therefore the idea occurred to her of putting the milk-rice in a golden dish. And bringing out a golden dish that was worth a hundred thousand, she took up the cooking-vessel and began to pour out the milk-rice. All the milk-rice rolled off like water from a lotus-leaf, and exactly filled the dish. Then, covering the dish with another, which was also made of gold, and wrapping it in a cloth, she adorned herself in all her ornaments, and with the dish on her head proceeded in state to the foot of the banyan-tree. As soon as she caught sight of the Future Buddha she was exceedingly overjoyed, supposing him to be the tree-god; and as she advanced she kept constantly bowing. And taking the pot from her head, she uncovered it, and with some flower-scented water in a golden vase, drew near and took up a position close to the Future Buddha. The earthenware bowl which the Future Buddha had kept so long, and which had been given him by Ghaṭīkāra, the Mahā-Brahma god, at that instant disappeared; and the Future Buddha, stretching out his right hand in an attempt to find his bowl, grasped the vase of water. Next Sujātā placed the dish of milk-rice in the hand of the Great

Being. Then the Great Being looked at Sujātā; and she perceived that he was a holy man, and did obeisance, and said, —

"Lord, accept my donation, and go whithersoever it seemeth to you good." And adding, "May your wishes prosper like mine own," she departed, caring no more for her golden dish worth a hundred thousand pieces of money than if it had been a dead leaf.

The Future Buddha rose from his seat and walked round the tree with his right side towards it; and taking the dish, he proceeded to the banks of the Nerañjarā and descended into its waters, just as many thousands of Future Buddhas before him had descended on the day of their complete enlightenment. — The spot where he bathed is now a place of pilgrimage named Suppatiṭṭhita, and here he deposited the dish on the bank before descending into the water. — After bathing he dressed himself in that garb of saintship which had been the dress of many hundreds of thousands of Future Buddhas before him; and sitting down with his face to the east, he made the whole of the thick, sweet milk-rice into forty-nine pellets of the size of the fruit of the single-seeded palmyra-tree, and ate it. And he took no further nourishment until the end of the seven weeks, or forty-nine days, which he spent on the throne of wisdom after he had become a Buddha. During all that time he had no other nourishment; he neither bathed, nor rinsed his mouth, nor did he ease himself; but was wholly taken up by the delights of the Trances, of the Paths, and of the Fruits.

Now when he had consumed the milk-rice, he took the golden dish; and saying, "If I am to succeed in becoming a Buddha to-day, let this dish go up-stream; but if not, let it go down-stream," he threw it into the water. And it swam, cleaving the stream, until it came to the middle of the river, and then, like a fleet horse, it ran up-stream for a distance of eighty cubits, keeping all the while in the middle of the stream. Then it dived into a whirlpool and went to the palace of the black snake-king, and hit, "click! click!" against the dishes that had been used by the last three Buddhas, and took its place at the end of the row. When the black snake-king heard the noise, he exclaimed, —

> "But yesterday a Buddha lived,
> And now another has been born."

and so on, through several hundred laudatory verses. As a matter of only yesterday and to-day did the times of the snake-king's appearance above ground seem to him; and his body at such times towered up into the sky to a height of one and three quarters leagues.

Then the Future Buddha took his noonday rest on the banks of the river, in a grove of sal-trees in full bloom. And at nightfall, at the time the flowers droop on their stalks, he rose up, like a lion when he bestirs himself, and went towards the Bo-tree, along a road which the gods had decked, and which was eight usabhas wide.

The snakes, the fairies, the birds, and other classes of beings did him homage with celestial perfumes, flowers, and other offerings, and celestial choruses poured forth heavenly music; so that the ten thousand worlds were filled with these perfumes, garlands, and shouts of acclaim.

Just then there came from the opposite direction a grass-cutter named Sotthiya, and he was carrying grass. And when he saw the Great Being, that he was a holy man, he gave him eight handfuls of grass. The Future Buddha took the grass, and ascending the throne of wisdom, stood on the southern side and faced the north. Instantly the southern half of the world sank, until it seemed to touch the Avīci hell, while the northern half rose to the highest of the heavens.

"Methinks," said the Future Buddha, "this cannot be the place for the attainment of the supreme wisdom;" and walking round the tree with his right side towards it, he came to the western side and faced the east. Then the western half of the world sank, until it seemed to touch the Avīci hell, while the eastern half rose to the highest of the heavens. Wherever, indeed, he stood, the broad earth rose and fell, as though it had been a huge cart-wheel lying on its hub, and some one were treading on the rim.

"Methinks," said the Future Buddha, "this also cannot be the place for the attainment of supreme wisdom;" and walking round the tree with his right side towards it, he came to the northern side and faced the south. Then the northern half of the world sank, until it seemed to touch the Avīci hell, while the southern half rose to the highest of the heavens.

"Methinks," said the Future Buddha, "this also cannot be the place for the attainment of supreme wisdom;" and walking round the tree with his right side towards it, he came to the eastern side and faced the west. Now it is on the eastern side of their Bo-trees that all The Buddhas have sat cross-legged, and that side neither trembles nor quakes.

Then the Great Being, saying to himself, "This is the immovable spot on which all The Buddhas have planted themselves! This is the place for destroying passion's net!" took hold of his handful of grass by one end, and shook it out there. And straightway the blades of grass formed themselves into a seat fourteen cubits long, of such symmetry of shape as not even the most skilful painter or carver could design.

Then the Future Buddha turned his back to the trunk of the Bo-tree and faced the east. And making the mighty resolution, "Let my skin, and sinews, and bones become dry, and welcome! and let all the flesh and blood in my body dry up! but never from this seat will I stir, until I have attained the supreme and absolute wisdom!" he sat himself down cross-legged in an unconquerable position, from which not even the descent of a hundred thunder-bolts at once could have dislodged him.

At this point the god Māra, exclaiming, "Prince Siddhattha is desirous of passing beyond my control, but I will never allow it!" went and announced the news to his army, and sounding the Māra war-cry, drew out for battle. Now Māra's army extended in front of him for twelve leagues, and to the right and to the left for twelve leagues, and in the rear as far as to the confines of the world, and it was nine leagues high. And when it shouted, it made an earthquake-like roaring and rumbling over a space of a thousand leagues. And the god Māra, mounting his elephant, which was a hundred and fifty leagues high, and had the name "Girded-with-mountains," caused a thousand arms to appear on his body, and with these he grasped a variety of weapons. Also in the remainder of that army, no two persons carried the same weapon; and diverse also in their appearances and countenances, the host swept on like a flood to overwhelm the Great Being.

Now deities throughout the ten thousand worlds were busy singing the praises of the Great Being. Sakka, the king of the gods, was blowing the conch-shell Vijayuttara. (This conch, they say, was a hundred and twenty cubits long, and when once it had been filled with wind, it would sound for four months before it stopped.) The great black snake-king sang more than a hundred laudatory verses. And Mahā-Brahma stood holding aloft the white umbrella. But as Māra's army gradually drew near to the throne of wisdom, not one of these gods was able to stand his ground, but each fled straight before him. The black snake-king dived into the ground, and coming to the snake-abode, Mañjerika, which was five hundred leagues in extent, he covered his face with both hands and lay down. Sakka slung his conch-shell Vijayuttara over his back, and took up his position on the rim of the world. Mahā-Brahma left the white umbrella at the end of the world, and fled to his Brahma-abode. Not a single deity was able to stand his ground, and the Great Being was left sitting alone.

Then said Māra to his followers, —

"My friends, Siddhattha, the son of Suddhodana, is far greater than any other man, and we shall never be able to fight him in front. We will attack him from behind."

All the gods had now disappeared, and the Great Being looked around on three sides, and said to himself, "There is no one here." Then looking to the north, he perceived Māra's army coming on like a flood, and said, —

"Here is this multitude exerting all their strength and power against me alone. My mother and father are not here, nor my brother, nor any other relative. But I have these Ten Perfections, like old retainers long cherished at my board. It therefore behooves me to make the Ten Perfections my shield and my sword, and to strike a blow with them that shall destroy this strong array." And he remained sitting, and reflected on the Ten Perfections.

Thereupon the god Māra caused a whirlwind, thinking, "By this will I drive away Siddhattha." Straightway the east wind and all the other different winds began to blow; but although these winds could have torn their way through mountain-peaks half a league, or two leagues, or three leagues high, or have uprooted forest-shrubs and trees, or have reduced to powder and scattered in all directions, villages and towns, yet when they reached the Future Buddha, such was the energy of the Great Being's merit, they lost all power and were not able to cause so much as a fluttering of the edge of his priestly robe.

Then he caused a great rain-storm, saying, "With water will I overwhelm and drown him." And through his mighty power, clouds of a hundred strata, and clouds of a thousand strata arose, and also the other different kinds. And these rained down, until the earth became gullied by the torrents of water which fell, and until the floods had risen over the tops of every forest-tree. But on coming to the Great Being, this mighty inundation was not able to wet his priestly robes as much as a dew-drop would have done.

Then he caused a shower of rocks, in which immense mountain-peaks flew smoking and flaming through the sky. But on reaching the Future Buddha they became celestial bouquets of flowers.

Then he caused a shower of weapons, in which single-edged, and double-edged swords, spears, and arrows flew smoking and flaming through the sky. But on reaching the Future Buddha they became celestial flowers.

Then he caused a shower of live coals, in which live coals as red as kiṁsuka flowers flew through the sky. But they scattered themselves at the Future Buddha's feet as a shower of celestial flowers.

Then he caused a shower of hot ashes, in which ashes that glowed like fire flew through the sky. But they fell at the Future Buddha's feet as sandal-wood powder.

Then he caused a shower of sand, in which very fine sand flew smoking and flaming through the sky. But it fell at the Future Buddha's feet as celestial flowers.

Then he caused a shower of mud, in which mud flew smoking and flaming through the sky. But it fell at the Future Buddha's feet as celestial ointment.

Then he caused a darkness, thinking, "By this will I frighten Siddhattha, and drive him away." And the darkness became fourfold, and very dense. But on reaching the Future Buddha it disappeared like darkness before the light of the sun.

Māra, being thus unable with these nine storms of wind, rain, rocks, weapons, live coals, hot ashes, sand, mud, and darkness, to drive away the Future Buddha, gave command to his followers, "Look ye now! Why stand ye still? Seize, kill, drive away this prince!" And, arming himself with a discus, and seated upon the shoulders of the elephant "Girded-with-mountains," he drew near the Future Buddha, and said, —

"Siddhattha, arise from this seat! It does not belong to you, but to me."

When the Great Being heard this he said, —

"Māra, you have not fulfilled the Ten Perfections in any of their three grades; nor have you made the five great donations;[1] nor have you striven for knowledge, nor for the welfare of the world, nor for enlightenment. This seat does not belong to you, but to me."

Unable to restrain his fury, the enraged Māra now hurled his discus. But the Great Being reflected on the Ten Perfections, and the discus changed into a canopy of flowers,

---

[1] These are the five donations great:
The gift of treasure, gift of child,
The gift of wife, of royal rule,
And last, the gift of life and limb.

From the *Abhidhānappadīpikā*, 421.

and remained suspended over his head. Yet they say that this keen-edged discus, when at other times Māra hurled it in anger, would cut through solid stone pillars as if they had been the tips of bamboo shoots. But on this occasion it became a canopy of flowers. Then the followers of Māra began hurling immense mountain-crags, saying, "This will make him get up from his seat and flee." But the Great Being kept his thoughts on the Ten Perfections, and the crags also became wreaths of flowers, and then fell to the ground.

Now the gods meanwhile were standing on the rim of the world, and craning their necks to look, saying, —

"Ah, woe the day! The handsome form of prince Siddhattha will surely be destroyed! What will he do to save himself?"

Then the Great Being, after his assertion that the seat which Future Buddhas had always used on the day of their complete enlightenment belonged to him, continued, and said, —

"Māra, who is witness to your having given donations?"

Said Māra, "All these, as many as you see here, are my witnesses;" and he stretched out his hand in the direction of his army. And instantly from Māra's army came a roar, "I am his witness! I am his witness!" which was like to the roar of an earthquake.

Then said Māra to the Great Being, —

"Siddhattha, who is witness to your having given donations?"

"Your witnesses," replied the Great Being, "are animate beings, and I have no animate witnesses present. However, not to mention the donations which I gave in other existences, the great seven-hundred-fold donation which I gave in my Vessantara existence shall now be testified to by the solid earth, inanimate though she be." And drawing forth his right hand from beneath his priestly robe, he stretched it out towards the mighty earth, and said, "Are you witness, or are you not, to my having given a great seven-hundred-fold donation in my Vessantara existence?"

And the mighty earth thundered, "I bear you witness!" with a hundred, a thousand, a hundred thousand roars, as if to overwhelm the army of Māra.

Now while the Great Being was thus calling to mind the donation he gave in his Vessantara existence, and saying to himself, "Siddhattha, that was a great and excellent donation which you gave," the hundred-and-fifty-league-high elephant "Girded-with-mountains" fell upon his knees before the Great Being. And the followers of Māra fled away in all directions. No two went the same way, but leaving their head-ornaments and their cloaks behind, they fled straight before them.

Then the hosts of the gods, when they saw the army of Māra flee, cried out, "Māra is defeated! Prince Siddhattha has conquered! Let us go celebrate the victory!" And the snakes egging on the snakes, the birds the birds, the deities the deities, and the Brahma-angels the Brahma-angels, they came with perfumes, garlands, and other offerings in their hands to the Great Being on the throne of wisdom. And as they came, —

274. "The victory now hath this illustrious Buddha won!
The Wicked One, the Slayer, hath defeated been!"
Thus round the throne of wisdom shouted joyously
The bands of snakes their songs of victory for the Sage;

275. "The victory now hath this illustrious Buddha won!
The Wicked One, the Slayer, hath defeated been!"
Thus round the throne of wisdom shouted joyously
The flocks of birds their songs of victory for the Sage;

276. "The victory now hath this illustrious Buddha won!
The Wicked One, the Slayer, hath defeated been!"
Thus round the throne of wisdom shouted joyously
The bands of gods their songs of victory for the Sage;

277. "The victory now hath this illustrious Buddha won!
The Wicked One, the Slayer, hath defeated been!"
Thus round the throne of wisdom shouted joyously
The Brahma-angels songs of victory for the Saint.

And the remaining deities, also, throughout the ten thousand worlds, made offerings of garlands, perfumes, and ointments, and in many a hymn extolled him.

It was before the sun had set that the Great Being thus vanquished the army of Māra. And then, while the Bo-tree in homage rained red, coral-like sprigs upon his priestly robes, he acquired in the first watch of the night the knowledge of previous existences; in the middle watch of the night, the divine eye; and in the last watch of the night, his intellect fathomed Dependent Origination.

Now while he was musing on the twelve terms of Dependent Origination, forwards and backwards, round and back again, the ten thousand worlds quaked twelve times, as far as to their ocean boundaries. And when the Great Being, at the dawning of the day, had thus made the ten thousand worlds thunder with his attainment of omniscience, all these worlds became most gloriously adorned. Flags and banners erected on the eastern rim of the world let their streamers fly to the western rim of the world; likewise those erected on the western rim of the world, to the eastern rim of the world; those erected on the northern rim of the world, to the southern rim of the world; and those erected on the southern rim of the world, to the northern rim of the world; while those erected on the level of the earth let theirs fly until they beat against the Brahma-world; and those of the Brahma-world let theirs hang down to the level of the earth. Throughout the ten thousand worlds the flowering trees bloomed; the fruit trees were weighted down by their burden of fruit; trunk-lotuses bloomed on the trunks of trees; branch-lotuses on the branches of trees; vine-lotuses on the vines; hanging-lotuses in the sky; and stalk-lotuses burst through the rocks and came up by sevens. The system of ten thousand worlds was like a bouquet of flowers sent whirling through the air, or like a thick carpet of flowers; in the intermundane spaces the eight-thousand-league-long hells, which not even the light of seven suns had formerly been able to illumine, were now flooded with radiance; the eighty-four-thousand-league-deep ocean became sweet to the taste; the rivers checked their flowing; the blind from birth received their sight; the deaf from birth their hearing; the cripples from birth the use of their limbs; and the bonds and fetters of captives broke and fell off.

When thus he had attained to omniscience, and was the centre of such unparalleled glory and homage, and so many prodigies were happening about him, he breathed forth that solemn utterance which has never been omitted by any of The Buddhas:—

> 278. "Through birth and rebirth's endless round,
> Seeking in vain, I hastened on,
> To find who framed this edifice.
> What misery! — birth incessantly!
>
> 279. "O builder! I've discovered thee!
> This fabric thou shalt ne'er rebuild!
> Thy rafters all are broken now,
> And pointed roof demolished lies!
> This mind has demolition reached,
> And seen the last of all desire!"

The period of time, therefore, from the existence in the Tusita Heaven to this attainment of omniscience on the throne of wisdom, constitutes the Intermediate Epoch.

---

§ 9. FIRST EVENTS AFTER THE ATTAINMENT OF BUDDHASHIP.

Translated from the Mahā-Vagga, and constituting the opening sections.

Hail to that Blessed One, that Saint, and Supreme Buddha!

AT that time The Buddha, The Blessed One, was dwelling at Uruvelā at the foot of the Bo-tree on the banks of the river Nerañjarā, having just attained the Buddhaship. Then The Blessed One sat cross-legged for seven days together at the foot of the Bo-tree experiencing the bliss of emancipation.

Then The Blessed One, during the first watch of the night, thought over Dependent Origination both forward and back: —

> On ignorance depends karma;
> On karma depends consciousness;
> On consciousness depend name and form;
> On name and form depend the six organs of sense;
> On the six organs of sense depends contact;
> On contact depends sensation;
> On sensation depends desire;
> On desire depends attachment;
> On attachment depends existence;
> On existence depends birth;
> On birth depend old age and death, sorrow, lamentation, misery, grief, and despair.

Thus does this entire aggregation of misery arise. But on the complete fading out and cessation of ignorance ceases karma; on the cessation of karma ceases consciousness; on the cessation of consciousness cease name and form; on the cessation of name and form cease the six organs of sense; on the cessation of the six organs of sense ceases contact; on the cessation of contact ceases sensation; on the cessation of sensation ceases desire; on the cessation of desire ceases attachment; on the cessation of attachment ceases existence; on the cessation of existence ceases birth; on the cessation of birth cease old age and death, sorrow, lamentation, misery, grief, and despair. Thus does this entire aggregation of misery cease.

Then The Blessed One, concerning this, on that occasion, breathed forth this solemn utterance, —

> "When to the strenuous, meditative Brahman
> There come to light the elements of being,
> Then vanish all his doubts and eager questions,
> What time he knows THE ELEMENTS HAVE CAUSES."

Then The Blessed One, during the middle watch of the

night, thought over Dependent Origination both forward and back: — On ignorance depends karma. . . . Thus does this entire aggregation of misery arise. But on the complete fading out and cessation of ignorance ceases karma. . . . Thus does this entire aggregation of misery cease.

Then The Blessed One, concerning this, on that occasion, breathed forth this solemn utterance, —

> "When to the strenuous, meditative Brahman
> There come to light the elements of being,
> Then vanish all his doubts and eager questions,
> What time he knows HOW CAUSES HAVE AN ENDING."

Then The Blessed One, during the last watch of the night, thought over Dependent Origination both forward and back: — On ignorance depends karma. . . . Thus does this entire aggregation of misery arise. But on the complete fading out and cessation of ignorance ceases karma. . . . Thus does this entire aggregation of misery cease.

Then The Blessed One, concerning this, on that occasion, breathed forth this solemn utterance, —

> "When to the strenuous, meditative Brahman
> There come to light the elements of being,
> Then scattereth he the hordes of Māra's army;
> Like to the sun that lightens all the heavens."

End of the account of what took place under the Bo-tree.

Then The Blessed One, after the lapse of seven days, arose from that state of exalted calm, and leaving the foot of the Bo-tree, drew near to where the Ajapāla (that is, the Goatherd's) banyan-tree was; and having drawn near, he sat cross-legged at the foot of the Ajapāla banyan-tree for seven days together, experiencing the bliss of emancipation.

Then a certain Brahman, who was of a proud and contemptuous disposition, drew near to where The Blessed One was; and having drawn near, he exchanged greetings with The Blessed One. And having passed with him the greetings of friendship and civility, he stood respectfully at one side. And standing respectfully at one side, the Brahman spoke to The Blessed One as follows: —

"Gotama, what is it constitutes a Brahman? and what are the Brahman-making qualities?"

Then The Blessed One, concerning this, on that occasion, breathed forth this solemn utterance, —

> "The Brahman who his evil traits hath banished,
> Is free from pride, is self-restrained and spotless,
> Is learnèd, and the holy life hath followed,
> 'T is he alone may claim the name of Brahman;
> With things of earth he hath no point of contact."

End of the account of what took place under the Ajapāla-tree.

Then The Blessed One, after the lapse of seven days, arose from that state of exalted calm, and leaving the foot of the Ajapāla banyan-tree, drew near to where the Mucalinda tree was; and having drawn near, he sat cross-legged at the foot of the Mucalinda tree for seven days together, experiencing the bliss of emancipation.

Now at that time a great cloud appeared out of season, and for seven days it was rainy, cloudy weather, with a cold wind. Then issued Mucalinda, the serpent-king, from his abode, and enveloping the body of The Blessed One seven times with his folds, spread his great hood above his head, saying, —

"Let neither cold nor heat, nor gnats, flies, wind, sunshine, nor creeping creatures come near The Blessed One!"

Then, when seven days had elapsed, and Mucalinda, the serpent-king, knew that the storm had broken up, and that the clouds had gone, he unwound his coils from the body of The Blessed One. And changing his natural appearance into that of a young man, he stood before The Blessed One, and with his joined hands to his forehead did reverence to The Blessed One.

Then The Blessed One, concerning this, on that occasion, breathed forth this solemn utterance, —

"How blest the happy solitude
Of him who hears and knows the truth!
How blest is harmlessness towards all,
And self-restraint towards living things!
How blest from passion to be free,
All sensuous joys to leave behind!
Yet far the highest bliss of all
To leave the pride which says, 'I am.'"

End of the account of what took place under the Mucalinda-tree.

---

§ 10. THE CONVERSION OF SĀRIPUTTA AND MOGGALLĀNA.[1]

Translated from the Mahā-Vagga (i.23¹).

Now at that time, Sañjaya, the wandering ascetic, was dwelling at Rājagaha in company with a large following of wandering ascetics, two hundred and fifty in number; and at that time Sāriputta and Moggallāna were leading the religious life under Sañjaya, the wandering ascetic. And they had made this compact: "That one of us who shall first attain to the deathless is to tell it to the other."

Then the venerable Assaji, having put on his tunic in the morning and taken his bowl and his robes, entered Rājagaha for alms, winning the minds of men with his advancing and his retiring, with his looking and his gazing, with his drawing in his arms and his stretching out his arms, and having his eyes cast down, and perfect in his deportment. And Sāriputta, the wandering ascetic, saw the venerable Assaji going the rounds of Rājagaha for alms, winning the minds of men with his advancing and his retiring, with his looking and

---

[1] Sāriputta and Moggallāna after their conversion became the two chief disciples of The Buddha. See page 16, Story of Sumedha, verse 77.

his gazing, with his drawing in his arms and his stretching out his arms, and having his eyes cast down, and perfect in his deportment. And when he had seen him, it occurred to him as follows: —

"This must be a priest who is either a saint already, or has entered the path which conducts to saintship. What if now I draw near to this priest, and ask him, 'To follow whom, brother, did you retire from the world? Who is your teacher? and whose doctrine do you approve?'"

Then it occurred to Sāriputta, the wandering ascetic, as follows: —

"It is not a fit time to ask this priest questions while he is inside the city, and going the rounds for alms. What if now I follow in the wake of this priest in the manner approved of for those who have requests to prefer?"

Then the venerable Assaji, after he had gone the rounds of Rājagaha and obtained alms, issued from the city; and Sāriputta, the wandering ascetic, drew near to where the venerable Assaji was; and having drawn near, he exchanged greetings with the venerable Assaji; and having passed with him the greetings of friendship and civility, he stood respectfully at one side. And standing respectfully at one side, Sāriputta, the wandering ascetic, spoke to the venerable Assaji as follows: —

"Placid, brother, are all your organs of sense; clear and bright is the color of your skin. To follow whom, brother, did you retire from the world? Who is your teacher? and whose doctrine do you approve?"

"Brother, there is a great Sakyaputta monk, one who has retired from the world out of the Sakya clan. To follow this Blessed One have I retired from the world, and this Blessed One is my teacher, and the Doctrine of this Blessed One do I approve."

"But what, venerable sir, is your teacher's doctrine? and what does he proclaim?"

"Brother, I am a novice and a new-comer, and the time is but short since I retired from the world under this Doctrine and Discipline. I am not able to expound to you the Doctrine at any great length, but I can tell you the substance of it in brief."

Then Sāriputta, the wandering ascetic, spoke to the venerable Assaji as follows: —

"So be it, brother. Whether little or much, tell it me. Tell me only the substance; it is the substance I want. Why should you make a long matter of it?"

Then the venerable Assaji recited to Sāriputta, the wandering ascetic, the following exposition of the Doctrine: —

> "The Buddha hath the causes told
> Of all things springing from a cause;
> And also how things cease to be —
> 'T is this the Mighty Monk proclaims."

On hearing this exposition of the Doctrine, there arose in the mind of Sāriputta, the wandering ascetic, a clear and distinct perception of the Doctrine that whatever is subject to origination is subject also to cessation. "If this is the Doctrine," said he, "then, indeed, have you reached the sorrowless state lost sight of and neglected for many myriads of world-cycles."

Then Sāriputta, the wandering ascetic, drew near to where Moggallāna, the wandering ascetic, was. And Moggallāna, the wandering ascetic, saw Sāriputta, the wandering ascetic, approaching from afar; and when he had seen him, he spoke to Sāriputta, the wandering ascetic, as follows: —

"Placid, brother, are all your organs of sense; clear and bright is the color of your skin. Brother, have you attained to the deathless?"

"Yea, brother, I have attained to the deathless."

"But how, brother, did you attain to the deathless?"

"Brother, just now I saw Assaji the priest going the rounds of Rājagaha for alms, winning the minds of men with his advancing and his retiring, with his looking and his gazing, with his drawing in his arms and his stretching out his arms, and having his eyes cast down, and perfect in his deportment; and when I had seen him, it occurred to me as follows: —

"This must be a priest who is either a saint already, or has entered the path which conducts to saintship. What if now I were to draw near to this priest, and ask him, 'To follow whom, brother, did you retire from the world? Who is your teacher? and whose doctrine do you approve?' Then, brother, it occurred to me as follows: 'It is not a fit time to ask this priest questions while he is inside the city and going the round for alms. What if now I follow in the wake of this priest in the manner approved of for those who have requests to prefer?' Then, brother, Assaji the priest, after he had gone the rounds of Rājagaha and obtained alms, issued from the city; and I, brother, drew near to where Assaji the priest was; and having drawn near, I exchanged greetings with the venerable Assaji; and having passed with him the greetings of friendship and civility, I stood respectfully at one side. And standing respectfully at one side, I spoke, brother, to the venerable Assaji as follows: 'Placid, brother, are all your organs of sense; clear and bright is the color of your skin. To follow whom, brother, did you retire from the world? Who is your teacher? and whose doctrine do you approve?' 'Brother, there is a great Sakyaputta monk, one who has retired from the world out of the Sakya clan. To follow this Blessed One have I retired from the world, and this Blessed One is my teacher, and the Doctrine of this Blessed One do I approve.' 'But what, venerable sir, is your teacher's doctrine? and what does he proclaim?' 'Brother, I am a novice and a new-comer, and the time is but short since I retired from the world under the Doctrine and Discipline. I am not able to expound to you the Doctrine at any great length, but I can tell you the substance of it in brief.' 'So be it, brother. Whether little or much, tell it me. Tell me only the substance; it is the substance I want. Why should you make a long matter of it?' Then, brother, Assaji the priest recited to me the following exposition of the Doctrine: —

"'The Buddha hath the causes told
Of all things springing from a cause;
And also how things cease to be —
'T is this the Mighty Monk proclaims.'"

On hearing this exposition of the Doctrine, there arose in the mind of Moggallāna, the wandering ascetic, a clear and distinct perception of the Doctrine that whatever is subject to origination is subject also to cessation. "If this is the Doctrine," said he, "then, indeed, have you reached the sorrowless state lost sight of and neglected for many myriads of world-cycles."

---

§ 11. THE BUDDHA'S DAILY HABITS.

Translated from the Sumañgala-Vilāsinī (i.45[10]), Buddhaghosa's Commentary on the Dīgha-Nikāya.

HABITS are of two kinds, the profitable, and the unprofitable. Of these, the unprofitable habits of The Blessed One had been extirpated by his attainment of saintship at the time he sat cross-legged under the Bo-tree. Profitable habits, however, remained to The Blessed One.

These were fivefold: his before-breakfast habits; his after-breakfast habits; his habits of the first watch of the night; his habits of the middle watch of the night; his habits of the last watch of the night.

His before-breakfast habits were as follows:—

The Blessed One would rise early in the morning, and when, out of kindness to his body-servant[1] and for the sake of bodily comfort, he had rinsed his mouth and otherwise cared for his person, he would sit retired until it was time to go begging. And when it came time, he would put on his tunic, girdle, and robes, and taking his bowl, he would enter the village or the town for alms. Sometimes he went alone, sometimes surrounded by a congregation of priests; sometimes without anything especial happening, sometimes with the accompaniment of many prodigies.

While, namely, the Lord of the World is entering for

[1] In order to give him a chance to acquire merit by waiting on a Buddha: compare page 99*d*.

alms, gentle winds clear the ground before him; the clouds let fall drops of water to lay the dust in his pathway, and then become a canopy over him; other winds bring flowers and scatter them in his path; elevations of ground depress themselves, and depressions elevate themselves; wherever he places his foot, the ground is even and pleasant to walk upon,[1] or lotus-flowers receive his tread. No sooner has he set his right foot within the city-gate than the rays of six different colors which issue from his body race hither and thither over palaces and pagodas, and deck them, as it were, with the yellow sheen of gold, or with the colors of a painting. The elephants, the horses, the birds, and other animals give forth melodious sounds; likewise the tom-toms, lutes, and other musical instruments, and the ornaments worn by the people.

By these tokens the people would know, "The Blessed One has now entered for alms;" and in their best tunics and best robes, with perfumes, flowers, and other offerings, they issue forth from their houses into the street. Then, having zealously paid homage to The Blessed One with the perfumes, flowers, and other offerings, and done him obeisance, some would implore him, "Reverend Sir, give us ten priests to feed;" some, "Give us twenty;" and some, "Give us a hundred priests." And they would take the bowl of The Blessed One, and prepare a seat for him, and zealously show their reverence for him by placing food in the bowl.

When he had finished his meal, The Blessed One, with due consideration for the different dispositions of their minds, would so teach them the Doctrine that some would become established in the refuges, some in the five precepts, some would become converted, some would attain to the fruit of either once returning, or of never returning, while some would become established in the highest fruit, that of saintship, and would retire from the world. Having shown this kindness to the multitude, he would rise from his seat, and return to the monastery.

---

[1] Compare Isaiah xl. 4: Every valley shall be exalted, and every mountain and hill shall be made low: . . . and the rough places plain.

On his arrival there, he would take his seat in a pavilion, on the excellent Buddha-mat which had been spread for him, where he would wait for the priests to finish their meal. When the priests had finished their meal, the body-servant would announce the fact to The Blessed One. Then The Blessed One would enter the perfumed chamber.

These, then, were his before-breakfast habits.

Then The Blessed One, having thus finished his before-breakfast duties, would first sit in the perfumed chamber, on a seat that had been spread for him by his body-servant, and would wash his feet. Then, taking up his stand on the landing of the jewelled staircase which led to the perfumed chamber, he would exhort the congregation of the priests, saying, —

"O priests, diligently work out your salvation; for not often occur the appearance of a Buddha in the world and existence among men[1] and the propitious moment and retirement from the world and the opportunity to hear the true Doctrine."

At this point some would ask The Blessed One for exercises in meditation, and The Blessed One would assign them exercises suited to their several characters. Then all would do obeisance to The Blessed One, and go to the places where they were in the habit of spending the night or the day — some to the forest, some to the foot of trees, some to the hills, and so on, some to the heaven of the four great kings, . . . and some to Vasavatti's heaven.

Then The Blessed One, entering the perfumed chamber, would, if he wished, lie down for a while, mindful and conscious, and on his right side after the manner of a lion. And secondly, his body being now refreshed, he would rise, and gaze over the world. And thirdly, the people of the village or town near which he might be dwelling, who had given him breakfast, would assemble after breakfast at the monastery, again in their best tunics and their best robes, and with perfumes, flowers, and other offerings.

---

[1] It is necessary to be a human being in order to attain to saintship, though gods can become converted and animals can keep the precepts. See pages 302, 279.

Thereupon The Blessed One, when his audience had assembled, would approach in such miraculous manner as was fitting; and taking his seat in the lecture-hall, on the excellent Buddha-mat which had been spread for him, he would teach the Doctrine, as suited the time and occasion. And when he perceived it was time, he would dismiss the audience, and the people would do obeisance to The Blessed One, and depart.

These were his after-breakfast habits.

When he had thus finished his after-breakfast duties, he would rise from the excellent Buddha-seat, and if he desired to bathe, he would enter the bath-house, and cool his limbs with water made ready by his body-servant. Then the body-servant would fetch the Buddha-seat, and spread it in the perfumed chamber. And The Blessed One, putting on a tunic of double red cloth, and binding on his girdle, and throwing his upper robe over his right shoulder, would go thither and sit down, and for a while remain solitary, and plunged in meditation. After that would come the priests from here and from there to wait on The Blessed One. And some would propound questions, some would ask for exercises in meditation, and some for a sermon; and in granting their desires The Blessed One would complete the first watch of the night.

These were his habits of the first watch of the night.

And now, when The Blessed One had finished his duties of the first watch of the night, and when the priests had done him obeisance and were departing, the deities throughout the entire system of ten thousand worlds would seize the opportunity to draw near to The Blessed One and ask him any questions that might occur to them, even such as were but four syllables long. And The Blessed One in answering their questions would complete the middle watch of the night.

These were his habits of the middle watch of the night.

The last watch of the night he would divide into three parts, and as his body would be tired from so much sitting since the morning, he would spend one part in pacing up and down to free himself from the discomfort. In the second part he would enter the perfumed chamber, and would lie down mindful and conscious, and on his right side after the manner of a lion. In the third part he would rise, and taking his seat, he would gaze over the world with the eye of a Buddha, in order to discover any individual who, under some former Buddha, with alms-giving, or keeping the precepts, or other meritorious deeds, might have made the earnest wish.

These were his habits of the last watch of the night.

---

§ 12. THE DEATH OF THE BUDDHA.

Translated from the Mahā-Parinibbāna-Sutta (v. and vi.) of the Dīgha-Nikāya.

THEN The Blessed One addressed the venerable Ānanda:—

"Let us go hence, Ānanda. To the further bank of the Hiraññavatī river, and to the city of Kusinārā and the sal-tree grove Upavattana of the Mallas will we draw near."

"Yes, Reverend Sir," said the venerable Ānanda to The Blessed One in assent.

Then The Blessed One, accompanied by a large congregation of priests, drew near to the further bank of the Hiraññavatī river, and to the city of Kusinārā and the sal-tree grove Upavattana of the Mallas; and having drawn near, he addressed the venerable Ānanda:—

"Be so good, Ānanda, as to spread me a couch with its head to the north between twin sal-trees. I am weary, Ānanda, and wish to lie down."

"Yes, Reverend Sir," said the venerable Ānanda to The Blessed One in assent, and spread the couch with its head to the north between twin sal-trees. Then The Blessed One lay down on his right side after the manner of a lion, and placing foot on foot, remained mindful and conscious.

Now at that time the twin sal-trees had completely burst forth into bloom, though it was not the flowering season;

and the blossoms scattered themselves over the body of The Tathāgata,[1] and strewed and sprinkled themselves in worship of The Tathāgata. Also heavenly Erythrina flowers fell from the sky; and these scattered themselves over the body of The Tathāgata, and strewed and sprinkled themselves in worship of The Tathāgata. Also heavenly sandal-wood powder fell from the sky; and this scattered itself over the body of The Tathāgata, and strewed and sprinkled itself in worship of The Tathāgata. And music sounded in the sky in worship of The Tathāgata, and heavenly choruses were heard to sing in worship of The Tathāgata.

Then The Blessed One addressed the venerable Ānanda: —

"The twin sal-trees, Ānanda, have completely burst forth into bloom, though it is not the flowering season; and the blossoms have scattered themselves over the body of The Tathāgata, and have strewn and sprinkled themselves in worship of The Tathāgata. Also heavenly Erythrina flowers have fallen from the sky; and these have scattered themselves over the body of The Tathāgata, and have strewn and sprinkled themselves in worship of The Tathāgata. Also heavenly sandal-wood powder has fallen from the sky; and this has scattered itself over the body of The Tathāgata, and has strewn and sprinkled itself in worship of The Tathāgata. Also music is sounding in the sky in worship of The Tathāgata, and heavenly choruses are heard to sing in worship of The Tathāgata. But it is not by all this, Ānanda, that The Tathāgata is honored, esteemed, revered, worshiped, or venerated; but the priest, Ānanda, or the priestess, or the lay disciple, or the female lay disciple, who shall fulfil all the greater and lesser duties, conducting himself with propriety and in accordance with the precepts, by him is The Tathāgata honored, esteemed, revered, and worshiped with the best of worship. Accordingly, Ānanda, train yourselves,

[1] Tathāgata is a term most commonly used by The Buddha in referring to himself. Its meaning, like that of its Jaina equivalent *Tatthagaya*, possibly is, "He who has arrived there (*tatra* or *tattha*), *i.e.* to emancipation *or* Nirvana." See "Sacred Books of the East," vol. xiii. p. 82.

and fulfil all the greater and lesser duties, and conduct yourselves with propriety and in accordance with the precepts."

Now at that time the venerable Upavāṇa was standing in front of The Blessed One, and fanning him. Then The Blessed One was harsh to the venerable Upavāṇa, saying,—

"Step aside, O priest; stand not in front of me."

Then it occurred to the venerable Ānanda as follows:—

"Here, this venerable Upavāṇa has for a long time been the body-servant of The Blessed One, and kept himself at his beck and call; yet, although his last moments are near, The Blessed One is harsh to the venerable Upavāṇa, saying, 'Step aside, O priest; stand not in front of me.' What, pray, was the reason, and what was the cause, that The Blessed One was harsh to the venerable Upavāṇa, saying, 'Step aside, O priest; stand not in front of me'?"

Then the venerable Ānanda spoke to The Blessed One as follows:—

"Reverend Sir, here this venerable Upavāṇa has for a long time been the body-servant of The Blessed One, and kept himself at his beck and call; yet, although his last moments are near, The Blessed One is harsh to the venerable Upavāṇa, saying, 'Step aside, O priest; stand not in front of me.' Reverend Sir, what, pray, was the reason, and what was the cause, that The Blessed One was harsh to the venerable Upavāṇa, saying, 'Step aside, O priest; stand not in front of me'?"

"Ānanda, almost all the deities throughout ten worlds have come together to behold The Tathāgata. For an extent, Ānanda, of twelve leagues about the city Kusinārā and the sal-tree grove Upavattana of the Mallas, there is not a spot of ground large enough to stick the point of a hair into, that is not pervaded by powerful deities. And these deities, Ānanda, are angered, saying, 'From afar have we come to behold The Tathāgata, for but seldom, and on rare occasions, does a Tathāgata, a saint, and Supreme Buddha arise in the world; and now, to-night, in the last watch, will The Tathāgata pass into Nirvana; but this powerful priest stands in front of The Blessed One, concealing him, and we have no chance to see The Tathāgata, although his last moments are near.' Thus, Ānanda, are these deities angered."

"What are the deities doing, Reverend Sir, whom The Blessed One perceives?"

"Some of the deities, Ānanda, are in the air with their minds engrossed by earthly things, and they let fly their hair and cry aloud, and stretch out their arms and cry aloud, and fall headlong to the ground and roll to and fro, saying, 'All too soon will The Blessed One pass into Nirvana; all too soon will The Happy One pass into Nirvana; all too soon will The Light of the World vanish from sight!' Some of the deities, Ānanda, are on the earth with their minds engrossed by earthly things, and they let fly their hair and cry aloud, and stretch out their arms and cry aloud, and fall headlong on the ground and roll to and fro, saying, 'All too soon will The Blessed One pass into Nirvana; all too soon will The Happy One pass into Nirvana; all too soon will The Light of the World vanish from sight.' But those deities which are free from passion, mindful and conscious, bear it patiently, saying, 'Transitory are all things. How is it possible [that whatever has been born, has come into being, and is organized and perishable, should not perish? That condition is not possible.]'"

. . . .

(Chapter v., page 53[16].)

Then the venerable Ānanda entered the monastery, and, leaning against the bolt of the door, he wept, saying, —

"Behold, I am but a learner and not yet perfect, and my Teacher is on the point of passing into Nirvana, he who was so compassionate to me."

Then The Blessed One addressed the priests: —

"Where, O priests, is Ānanda?"

"Reverend Sir, the venerable Ānanda has entered the monastery, and leaning against the bolt of the door, he weeps, saying, 'Behold, I am but a learner, and not yet perfect, and my Teacher is on the point of passing into Nirvana, he who was so compassionate to me.'"

Then The Blessed One addressed a certain priest, saying, —

"Go, O priest, and say to the venerable Ānanda from me, 'The Teacher calleth thee, brother Ānanda.'"

"Yes, Reverend Sir," said the priest to The Blessed One in assent, and drew near to where the venerable Ānanda was; and having drawn near, he spoke to the venerable Ānanda as follows: —

"The Teacher calleth thee, brother Ānanda."

"Yes, brother," said the venerable Ānanda to the priest in assent, and drew near to where The Blessed One was; and having drawn near and greeted The Blessed One, he sat down respectfully at one side. And the venerable Ānanda being seated respectfully at one side, The Blessed One spoke to him as follows: —

"Enough, Ānanda, do not grieve, nor weep. Have I not already told you, Ānanda, that it is in the very nature of all things near and dear unto us that we must divide ourselves from them, leave them, sever ourselves from them? How is it possible, Ānanda, that whatever has been born, has come into being, is organized and perishable, should not perish? That condition is not possible. For a long time, Ānanda, have you waited on The Tathāgata with a kind, devoted, cheerful, single-hearted, unstinted service of body, with a kind, devoted, cheerful, single-hearted, unstinted service of voice, with a kind, devoted, cheerful, single-hearted, unstinted service of mind. You have acquired much merit, Ānanda; exert yourself, and soon will you be free from all depravity."

Then The Blessed One addressed the priests: —

"Priests, of all those Blessed Ones who aforetime were saints and Supreme Buddhas, all had their favorite body-servants, just as I have now my Ānanda. And, priests, of all those Blessed Ones who in the future shall be saints and Supreme Buddhas, all will have their favorite body-servants, just as I have now my Ānanda. Wise, O priests, is Ānanda — he knows when it is a fit time to draw near to see The Tathāgata, whether for the priests, for the priestesses, for the lay disciples, for the female lay disciples, for the king, for the king's courtiers, for the leaders of heretical sects, or for their adherents.

"Ānanda, O priests, has four wonderful and marvellous qualities. And what are the four? O priests, if an assembly of priests draw near to behold Ānanda, it is delighted with beholding him; and if then Ānanda hold a discourse on the Doctrine, it is also delighted with the discourse; and when Ānanda, O priests, ceases to speak, the assembly of priests is still unsated. O priests, if an assembly of priestesses . . . an assembly of lay disciples . . . an assembly of female lay disciples draw near to behold Ānanda, it is delighted with beholding him; and if then Ānanda hold a discourse on the Doctrine, it is also delighted with the discourse; and when Ānanda, O priests, ceases to speak, the assembly of female lay disciples is still unsated.

"A Universal Monarch, O priests, has four wonderful and marvellous qualities. And what are the four? O priests, if an assembly of men of the warrior caste . . . an assembly of men of the Brahman caste . . . an assembly of householders . . . an assembly of monks draw near to behold the Universal Monarch, it is delighted with beholding him; and if then the Universal Monarch hold a discourse, it is also delighted with the discourse; and when the Universal Monarch, O priests, ceases to speak, the assembly of monks is still unsated.

"In exactly the same way, O priests, Ānanda has four wonderful and marvellous qualities. O priests, if an assembly of priests . . . an assembly of priestesses . . . an assembly of lay disciples . . . an assembly of female lay disciples draw near to behold Ānanda, it is delighted with beholding him; and if then Ānanda hold a discourse on the Doctrine, it is also delighted with the discourse; and when Ānanda, O priests, ceases to speak, the assembly of female lay disciples is still unsated. These, O priests, are the four wonderful and marvellous qualities possessed by Ānanda."

When The Blessed One had thus spoken, the venerable Ānanda spoke to him as follows: —

"Reverend Sir, let not The Blessed One pass into Nirvana

in this wattel-and-daub town, this town of the jungle, this branch village. For there are other great cities, Reverend Sir, to wit, Campā, Rājagaha, Sāvatthi, Sāketa, Kosambī, and Benares. Let The Blessed One pass into Nirvana in one of them. In them are many wealthy men of the warrior caste, many wealthy men of the Brahman caste, and many wealthy householders who are firm believers in The Tathāgata, and they will perform the funeral rites for The Tathāgata."

"O Ānanda, say not so! O Ānanda, say not so, that this is a wattel-and-daub town, a town of the jungle, a branch village. There was once, Ānanda, a king called Sudassana the Great, who was a Universal Monarch, a virtuous king of justice, a victorious ruler of the four quarters of the earth, possessing a secure dominion over his territory and owning the seven precious gems.[1] This city Kusinārā, Ānanda, was the capital of king Sudassana the Great, and had then the name of Kusāvatī. From the east to the west it was twelve leagues in length, and from the north to the south it was seven leagues in breadth. Kusāvatī, the capital, Ānanda, was prosperous and flourishing, populous and thronging with people, and well provided with food. As Āḷakamandā, the capital of the gods, Ānanda, is prosperous and flourishing, populous and thronging with gods, and is well provided with food, in exactly the same way, Ānanda, Kusāvatī, the capital, was prosperous and flourishing, populous and thronging with people, and well provided with food. Kusāvatī, the capital, Ānanda, was neither by day nor night without the ten noises, — to wit, the noise of elephants, the noise of horses, the noise of chariots, the noise of drums, the noise of tabors, the noise of lutes, the noise of song, the noise of cymbals, the noise of gongs, and the tenth noise of people crying, 'Eat ye, and drink!'

"Go thou, Ānanda, and enter the city Kusinārā, and announce to the Kusinārā-Mallas: —

"'To-night, O ye Vāseṭṭhas, in the last watch, The

[1] The wheel of empire, the elephant, the horse, the gem, the empress, the treasurer, and the crown-prince.

Tathāgata will pass into Nirvana. Be favorable, be favorable, O ye Vāseṭṭhas, and suffer not that afterwards ye feel remorse, saying, "The Tathāgata passed into Nirvana while in our borders, but we did not avail ourselves of the opportunity of being present at the last moments of The Tathāgata."'"

"Yes, Reverend Sir," said the venerable Ānanda to The Blessed One in assent; and putting on his tunic, and taking his bowl and his robes, he went to Kusinārā with another member of the Order.

Now at that time the Kusinārā-Mallas were assembled together in the town-hall on some matter of business. And the venerable Ānanda drew near to the town-hall of the Kusinārā-Mallas; and having drawn near, he made announcement to the Kusinārā-Mallas, as follows: —

"To-night, O ye Vāseṭṭhas, in the last watch, The Tathāgata will pass into Nirvana. Be favorable, be favorable, O ye Vāseṭṭhas, and suffer not that afterwards ye feel remorse, saying, 'The Tathāgata passed into Nirvana while in our borders, but we did not avail ourselves of the opportunity of being present at the last moments of The Tathāgata.'"

The Mallas, on hearing this speech of the venerable Ānanda, and their children and their daughters-in-law and their wives were grieved and sorrowful and overwhelmed with anguish of mind, and some let fly their hair and cried aloud, and stretched out their arms and cried aloud, and fell headlong to the ground and rolled to and fro, saying, "All too soon will The Blessed One pass into Nirvana; all too soon will The Happy One pass into Nirvana; all too soon will The Light of the World vanish from sight." Then the Mallas and their children and their daughters-in-law and their wives, being grieved and sorrowful and overwhelmed with anguish of mind, drew near to the sal-tree grove Upavattana of the Mallas, and to where the venerable Ānanda was.

Then it occurred to the venerable Ānanda as follows: —

"If I shall cause the Kusinārā-Mallas one by one to do reverence to The Blessed One, the day will dawn ere they have finished. What if now I marshal the Mallas by families, and cause them by families to do reverence to The Blessed One, and say, 'Reverend Sir, a Malla named so-and-so, with his children, his wife, his following, and his friends, bows low in reverence at the feet of The Blessed One.' "

And the venerable Ānanda marshalled the Mallas by families, and caused them by families to do reverence to The Blessed One, saying, "Reverend Sir, a Malla named so-and-so, with his children, his wife, his following, and his friends, bows low in reverence at the feet of The Blessed One." And the venerable Ānanda by this device succeeded in causing all the Kusinārā-Mallas to do reverence to The Blessed One before the end of the first watch of the night.

Now at that time Subhadda, a wandering ascetic, was dwelling at Kusinārā. And Subhadda, the wandering ascetic, heard the report: —

"To-night, in the last watch, the monk Gotama will pass into Nirvana."

Then it occurred to Subhadda, the wandering ascetic, as follows: —

"I have heard wandering ascetics, that were old men, advanced in years, teachers, and teachers' teachers, declare, 'But seldom, and on rare occasions, does a Tathāgata, a saint, and Supreme Buddha arise in the world.' And to-night, in the last watch, the monk Gotama will pass into Nirvana. And a certain question has arisen in my mind, and I am persuaded of the monk Gotama that he can so teach me the Doctrine that I shall be relieved of this my doubt."

Then Subhadda, the wandering ascetic, drew near to the sal-tree grove Upavattana of the Mallas, and to where the venerable Ānanda was, and having drawn near, he spoke to the venerable Ānanda as follows: —

"Ānanda, I have heard wandering ascetics, that were old men, advanced in years, teachers, and teachers' teachers, declare, 'But seldom, and on rare occasions, does a Tathāgata, a saint, and Supreme Buddha arise in the world.' And to-night, in the last watch, the monk Gotama will pass into Nirvana. And a certain doubt has arisen in my mind, and I am persuaded of the monk Gotama that he can so teach me the Doctrine that I shall be relieved of this my doubt. Let me, then, Ānanda, have an opportunity of seeing the monk Gotama."

When Subhadda, the wandering ascetic, had so spoken, the venerable Ānanda spoke to him as follows: —

"Enough of that, brother Subhadda; trouble not The Tathāgata. The Blessed One is weary."

And a second time Subhadda, the wandering ascetic, . . .

And a third time Subhadda, the wandering ascetic, spoke to the venerable Ānanda as follows: —

"Ānanda, I have heard wandering ascetics, old men, advanced in years, teachers, and teachers' teachers, when they said, 'But seldom, and on rare occasions, does a Tathāgata, a saint, and Supreme Buddha arise in the world.' And to-night, in the last watch, the monk Gotama will pass into Nirvana. And a certain doubt has arisen in my mind, and I am persuaded of the monk Gotama that he can so teach me the Doctrine that I shall be relieved of this my doubt. Let me, then, Ānanda, have an opportunity of seeing the monk Gotama."

And a third time the venerable Ānanda spoke to Subhadda, the wandering ascetic, as follows: —

"Enough of that, brother Subhadda; trouble not The Tathāgata. The Blessed One is weary."

Now The Blessed One chanced to hear the conversation between the venerable Ānanda and the wandering ascetic Subhadda. And The Blessed One called to the venerable Ānanda: —

"Enough, Ānanda; hinder not Subhadda. Let Subhadda, Ānanda, have an opportunity of beholding The Tathāgata. Whatever Subhadda shall ask of me, he will ask for the sake of information, and not for the sake of troubling me, and he will quickly understand my answers to his questions."

Then the venerable Ānanda spoke to Subhadda, the wandering ascetic, as follows: —

"You may come, brother Subhadda; The Blessed One grants you an audience."

Then Subhadda, the wandering ascetic, drew near to

where The Blessed One was; and having drawn near, he exchanged greetings with The Blessed One; and having passed with him the greetings of friendship and civility, he sat down respectfully at one side. And seated respectfully at one side, Subhadda, the wandering ascetic, spoke to The Blessed One as follows: —

"Gotama, all those monks and Brahmans who possess a large following and crowds of hearers and disciples, and who are distinguished, renowned leaders of sects, and highly esteemed by the multitudes, — to wit, Pūraṇa Kassapa, Makkhali Gosāla, Ajita Kesakambali, Pakudha Kaccāyana, Sañjaya Belaṭṭhiputta, Nigaṇṭha Nāthaputta, — have they all done as they maintain, discovered the truth, or have they not? or have some of them done so, and others not?"

"Enough, O Subhadda; let us leave the question, 'Have they all done as they maintain, discovered the truth, or have they not? or have some of them done so, and others not?' The Doctrine will I teach you, Subhadda. Listen to me, and pay strict attention, and I will speak."

"Yes, Reverend Sir," said Subhadda, the wandering ascetic, to The Blessed One in assent. And The Blessed One spoke as follows: —

"Subhadda, in whatever doctrine and discipline the noble eightfold path is not found, therein also is not found the monk of the first degree, nor the monk of the second degree, nor the monk of the third degree, nor the monk of the fourth degree; and in whatever doctrine and discipline, O Subhadda, the noble eightfold path is found, therein also are found the monk of the first degree, and the monk of the second degree, and the monk of the third degree, and the monk of the fourth degree. Now in this Doctrine and Discipline, O Subhadda, the noble eightfold path is found: and therein alone, O Subhadda, are found the monk of the first degree, and the monk of the second degree, and the monk of the third degree, and the monk of the fourth degree. Destitute of true monks are all other creeds. But let these my priests, O Subhadda, live rightly, and the world will not be destitute of saints.

"What time my age was twenty-nine, Subhadda,
I left the world to seek the summum bonum.
Now fifty years and more have passed, Subhadda,
Since I renounced the world and lived ascetic
Within the Doctrine's pale, that rule of conduct
Outside of which no genuine monk existeth,

nor the monk of the second degree, nor the monk of the third degree, nor the monk of the fourth degree. Destitute of monks are all other creeds. But let these my priests, O Subhadda, live rightly, and the world will not be destitute of saints."

When The Blessed One had thus spoken, Subhadda, the wandering ascetic, spoke to him as follows:—

"O wonderful is it, Reverend Sir! O wonderful is it, Reverend Sir! It is as if, Reverend Sir, one were to set up that which was overturned, or were to disclose that which was hidden, or were to point out the way to a lost traveller, or were to carry a lamp into a dark place that they who had eyes might see forms. Even so has The Blessed One expounded the Doctrine in many different ways. Reverend Sir, I betake myself to The Blessed One for refuge, to the Doctrine, and to the Congregation of the priests. Suffer me to retire from the world under The Blessed One; suffer me to receive ordination."

"Subhadda, any one who aforetime has been an adherent of another sect and afterwards desires to retire from the world and receive ordination under this Doctrine and Discipline, must first spend four months on probation; and after the lapse of four months, strenuous-minded priests receive him into the Order and confer on him the priestly ordination. Nevertheless, in this matter of probation I recognize a difference in persons."

"Reverend Sir, if all they who aforetime have been adherents of other sects and afterwards desire to retire from the world and receive ordination under this Doctrine and Discipline, must first spend four months on probation, and after the lapse of four months strenuous-minded priests receive them into the Order, and confer on them the priestly ordination, then am I ready to spend four years on probation, and after the lapse of four years, let strenuous-minded priests receive me into the Order and confer on me the priestly ordination."

Then The Blessed One said to the venerable Ānanda,

"Well, then, Ānanda, receive Subhadda into the Order."

"Yes, Reverend Sir," said the venerable Ānanda to The Blessed One in assent.

Then Subhadda, the wandering ascetic, spoke to the venerable Ānanda as follows:—

"How fortunate you priests are, brother Ānanda! How supremely fortunate, brother Ānanda, that you all have been sprinkled with the sprinkling of discipleship at the hands of The Teacher himself."

And Subhadda, the wandering ascetic, retired from the world under The Blessed One, and received ordination. And without delay, after he had received ordination, the venerable Subhadda began to live solitary and retired, vigilant, strenuous, and zealous; and in no long time, and while yet alive, he came to learn for himself, and to realize, and to live in the possession of that highest good to which the holy life conducts, and for the sake of which youths of good family so nobly retire from the household life to the houseless one. And he knew that for him rebirth was exhausted, that he had lived the holy life, that he had done what it behooved him to do, and that he was no more for this world. So the venerable Subhadda became of the number of the saints, and he was the last disciple made by The Blessed One himself.

End of the Hiraññavatī Recitation, which is the Fifth.

Then The Blessed One addressed the venerable Ānanda:—

"It may be, Ānanda, that some of you will think, 'The word of The Teacher is a thing of the past; we have now no Teacher.' But that, Ānanda, is not the correct view. The Doctrine and Discipline, Ānanda, which I have taught and enjoined upon you is to be your teacher when I am gone. But whereas now, Ānanda, all the priests address each other with the title of 'brother,' not so must they address each other after I am gone. A senior priest, Ānanda, is to address a junior priest either by his given name, or by his family name, or by the title of 'brother;' a junior priest is to address a senior priest with the title 'reverend sir,' or 'venerable.' If the Order, Ānanda, wish to do so, after I am gone they may abrogate all the lesser and minor precepts. On Channa,[1] Ānanda, after I am gone, the higher penalty is to be inflicted."

"Reverend Sir, what is this higher penalty?"

"Let Channa, Ānanda, say what he likes, he is not to be spoken to nor admonished nor instructed by the priests."

Then The Blessed One addressed the priests:—

"It may be, O priests, that some priest has a doubt or perplexity respecting either The Buddha or the Doctrine or the Order or the Path or the course of conduct. Ask any questions, O priests, and suffer not that afterwards ye feel remorse, saying, 'Our Teacher was present with us, but we failed to ask him all our questions.'"

When he had so spoken, the priests remained silent.

And a second time The Blessed One, and a third time The Blessed One addressed the priests:—

"It may be, O priests, that some priest has a doubt or perplexity respecting either The Buddha or the Doctrine or the Order or the Path or the course of conduct. Ask any question, O priests, and suffer not that afterwards ye feel remorse, saying, 'Our Teacher was present with us, but we failed to ask him all our questions.'"

And a third time the priests remained silent.

Then The Blessed One addressed the priests:—

"It may be, O priests, that it is out of respect to The Teacher that ye ask no questions. Then let each one speak to his friend."

And when he had thus spoken, the priests remained silent.

Then the venerable Ānanda spoke to The Blessed One as follows:—

"It is wonderful, Reverend Sir! It is marvellous, Rev-

[1] Not the Channa who had been the Future Buddha's charioteer.

erend Sir! Reverend Sir, I have faith to believe that in this congregation of priests not a single priest has a doubt or perplexity respecting either The Buddha or the Doctrine or the Order or the Path or the course of conduct."

"With you, Ānanda, it is a matter of faith, when you say that; but with The Tathāgata, Ānanda, it is a matter of knowledge that in this congregation of priests not a single priest has a doubt or perplexity respecting either The Buddha or the Doctrine or the Order or the Path or the course of conduct. For of all these five hundred priests, Ānanda, the most backward one has become converted, and is not liable to pass into a lower state of existence, but is destined necessarily to attain supreme wisdom."

Then The Blessed One addressed the priests: —

"And now, O priests, I take my leave of you; all the constituents of being are transitory; work out your salvation with diligence."

And this was the last word of The Tathāgata.

Thereupon The Blessed One entered the first trance; and rising from the first trance, he entered the second trance; and rising from the second trance, he entered the third trance; and rising from the third trance, he entered the fourth trance; and rising from the fourth trance, he entered the realm of the infinity of space; and rising from the realm of the infinity of space, he entered the realm of the infinity of consciousness; and rising from the realm of the infinity of consciousness, he entered the realm of nothingness; and rising from the realm of nothingness, he entered the realm of neither perception nor yet non-perception; and rising from the realm of neither perception nor yet non-perception, he arrived at the cessation of perception and sensation.

Thereupon the venerable Ānanda spoke to the venerable Anuruddha as follows: —

"Reverend Anuruddha, The Blessed One has passed into Nirvana."

"Nay, brother Ānanda, The Blessed One has not passed into Nirvana; he has arrived at the cessation of perception and sensation."

Thereupon The Blessed One rising from the cessation of his perception and sensation, entered the realm of neither perception nor yet non-perception; and rising from the realm of neither perception nor yet non-perception, he entered the realm of nothingness; and rising from the realm of nothingness, he entered the realm of the infinity of consciousness; and rising from the realm of the infinity of consciousness, he entered the realm of the infinity of space; and rising from the realm of the infinity of space, he entered the fourth trance; and rising from the fourth trance, he entered the third trance; and rising from the third trance, he entered the second trance; and rising from the second trance, he entered the first trance; and rising from the first trance, he entered the second trance; and rising from the second trance, he entered the third trance; and rising from the third trance, he entered the fourth trance; and rising from the fourth trance, immediately The Blessed One passed into Nirvana.